MORE THAN GUIDED READING

MORE THAN THAN GUIDED READING

Finding the Right Instructional Mix, K–3

CATHY MERE

FOREWORD BY MAX BRAND

STENHOUSE PUBLISHERS
PORTLAND, MAINE

Stenhouse Publishers
www.stenhouse.com

Library of Congress Cataloging-in-Publication Data
Mere, Cathy, 1966–
    More than guided reading: finding the right instructional mix, K–3 / by Cathy Mere.
        p. cm.
    Includes bibliographical references.
    ISBN 1-57110-388-0
    1. Guided reading. 2. Children—Books and reading. I. Title.

    LB1050.377.M47 2005
    372.41'62—dc22   2005049986

Cover and interior design by Catherine Hawkes, Cat & Mouse
Typeset by Cat & Mouse

Manufactured in the United States of America on acid-free paper
10 09   9 8 7 6 5 4 3

In memory of my grandfather, Dwight Pierce,
who first taught me about apprenticeship,
side by side, in his workshop.

TABLE OF CONTENTS

I first met Cathy Mere seven years ago while I was a district-level literacy coach. I was teaching a guided-reading lesson for first graders while being observed by a dozen literacy coaches and teachers. Cathy had heard about our literacy project and asked to participate. She was curious about finding a way to integrate her Reading Recovery knowledge with her classroom practices.

That first encounter is still vivid in my mind. What sticks with me are Cathy's questions, questions that resonate throughout this book:

What is the role of guided reading within a balanced literacy framework?
Do reading groups force us to teach to the middle ground, or is there a
    way to tailor them to individual students' needs?
How do we teach *readers* as well as reading?

I still remember that first encounter because Cathy's questions were well crafted, designed to probe the deeper thinking behind my surface teaching. They all led back, one way or another, to the function of guided-reading groups in primary classrooms. That meeting was the start of many years of collaboration between us as literacy coaches in the Hilliard, Ohio, public schools. The longer I have known Cathy, the more I respect her. Our conversations push me to revise my thinking, just as her conversations with colleagues and with children extend their literacy learning.

Guided-reading groups have become the centerpiece of reading instruction in primary grades, and it is time to address what is gained and what is lost by their prominence. Through her attempts to address this issue in her classroom, Cathy's teaching has changed. She now devotes less time to guided reading, which frees her to extend conversations from read-aloud and focused lessons to individual or whole-group settings. This seamless instruction allows her to meet the needs of individual students outside of guided-reading groups. In this book we have the opportunity to meet Marcie, Tori, Billy, Emily, Tamarah, Kanna, and Nazarena as

Cathy thinks through her teaching moves, tailoring instruction for these children and never losing sight of what it means to be literate.

In *More Than Guided Reading*, Cathy invites us all to rethink what we mean by "balance" in reading programs by showing us the importance of oral language and purposeful conversation. Helping students develop a vocabulary for talking about books expands their vocabulary for talking about the world. These skills are necessary for membership in what Frank Smith calls "the literacy club." Her read-alouds, paired with focus lessons, help learners (including many English-language learners) to cultivate a sense of story, to fall in love with books, to encounter a variety of authors, and to discover the power of language. Perhaps most of all, Cathy reminds us of the importance of *listening* to students. While her students speak, Cathy is learning about them as thinkers and readers.

After reading Cathy's thoughtful book, I want to return to teaching in primary grades, especially first grade. I want the chance to borrow from Cathy's thinking so that I too can help novice readers become members of "the literacy club." We are fortunate to have a book that captures Cathy's reflections, curiosity, and passion for learning. *More Than Guided Reading* offers a chance to peek into the mind of a master teacher as she reworks her theories and practices in the midst of her reading instruction.

Max Brand

Voice is often associated with writing, but it is also a significant part of teaching. Through my work as a literacy coach I have been able to spend time in many classrooms. In these communities, I have discovered the rhythm and tone created by the teacher's voice as he or she crafts instruction and interacts with children. My journey has been to find my own teaching voice, the one with which I am comfortable in the classroom. Many conversations along the way have become a part of my thinking and are reflected within these pages.

Time and place can be everything, and I have been fortunate to work with many outstanding educational leaders who have helped to shape my voice along the way. Max Brand has stretched my thinking and helped me to put children at the center of my decision making; most important, he has put up with my persistent barrage of questions. Cheri Slinger has taught me not only about supporting readers in a Reading Recovery lesson, but about pushing myself to find ways to help students to be successful. Through her I have learned the importance of explicit language and demonstration, the necessity of following students closely, and the power of praise.

I am thankful for those who have walked beside me on my journey, sharing their thoughts and challenging my thinking. Conversations with Jennifer Morgan, Deb Frazier, and Lisa Potts have not only energized my teaching, but left me with more questions than answers. Tonya Buelow, Molly Dickman, Sharon Esswein, Jeanne Falter, Kelly Hoenie, Tony Keefer, Debbie Lairson, Adrianna Mort, Marsha Pfahl, Teresa Scholl, Kevin Schulze, Sandy Smeenk, and Christy Tingley make a dynamic think tank of literacy specialists in Hilliard city schools, all bringing their own individual gifts to the table, strengthening professional development and ultimately making Hilliard an exciting place to teach and learn.

In addition, my voice has been influenced by the numerous colleagues and students I have had the privilege to spend time alongside in Jefferson local schools and Hilliard city schools. Thanks to all of the teachers who have opened their classrooms, paused for hallway chats, asked thoughtful questions, and taught me so much about working with children, especially Michelle Watts and Colleen Csiszarik, who went above and beyond the call of duty in allowing me to teach, photograph, and learn in their classrooms.

Juggling a classroom, a family, and the responsibilities of working as a literacy coach often made writing this book even more of a challenge. Where would I be without Amy Smedley? Her white magic has carried me through the hardest of times. Thanks also to Emilie Parker, whose response to my early writing first helped me to believe I might have something to say and whose thoughtful reflection helped me to begin. I have persevered. Jennifer Watson's early words helped me to find direction. Karen VanVleet, Cathi Elliott, and Liz Deskins provided the perfect words of encouragement when I needed them most.

Brenda Power has been instrumental in helping me to share the story of my journey. She has pushed when I needed it, listened when I needed an ear, guided when I needed focus, and provided a laugh at crucial moments. Her patience, thoughtful responses, and vision have helped me along the way. Thank-you also to Philippa Stratton, Jay Kilburn, Doug Kolmar, Linda Howe, and everyone at Stenhouse who has helped make this book a reality.

I would be remiss if I did not acknowledge the authors who have influenced my thinking and whose voices have become a part of all I do in my classroom. Debbie Miller has been an inspiration, making me think differently about my teaching and sharing the challenges of writing. Franki Sibberson somehow thought I might be able to do this. Her work with Karen Szymusiak, along with the words of Katie Wood Ray, Regie Routman, Gay Su Pinnell, Don Holdaway, Shelley Harwayne, Mem Fox, Irene Fountas, Ralph Fletcher, and Lucy Calkins, have sustained me.

When you agree to write a book, your whole family agrees to write a book. My husband, Jeff, and my children, Cortney, John, and Cassidy, have hung in there through countless working weekends and evenings. Thank-you to my parents, Sharon Slavik and Chuck Hilliker, as well as to Chad, Rob, Lisa, Anita, and Bob, who offered words of encouragement and always believed I could do it. My voice is stronger because of all of you.

CHAPTER 1

What Balance?

A scary thing happened today. I walked into our teachers' lounge, where the remnants of the secretaries' breakfast had been spread across the table, with the expectation that someone in the building would eat everything before the day came to an end, Atkins diet or not. On the back of the door someone had taped thirty-four lovely dolphins, intended to begin the countdown to the end of the school year, for most, a message of joy. I, however, was panicked. Only thirty-four days?

I thought back to the second week of school. I had been in my classroom preparing for the next day. Things had finally slowed down from the busy hustle and bustle of the first few days. My kindergarteners were not crying when they came in anymore. All twenty-six kids seemed to be able to get to their bus at the end of the day without incident. Carlos had finally quit carrying the photograph of his mother around the room while muttering, "My life is not the same without my mom." Life was good. I finally had time to read the bulletin board parents had created the night of open house telling me what they wanted their children to accomplish in kindergarten. The overwhelming response was, "Learn to read."

My stomach turned as I recalled reading those responses and wondering what parents meant by "learn to read." These kids were five- and six-year-olds in a half-day kindergarten program. Did their parents expect them to be reading novels by the end of the year? During this first year of school, according to my plans, students would learn to use some beginning reading strategies while reading for understanding as a class, in small groups and pairs, and individually. Together we would work to expand their oral language, cultivate their sense of story, and develop their phonemic awareness through authentic literacy experiences. We would surround ourselves with the voices of authors, voices that would help us to fall in love with their books.

I didn't expect kindergarten students to read novels, but I did expect them to discover how literacy worked in their world. I hoped they would become, as Frank

Smith terms it, a part of the "literacy club." As members of this club, the children in my classroom would be welcomed into our community of readers, no matter what their level of experience. Through regular opportunities to spend time with print, they would come to understand the role of written language in their lives. They would learn to read with purpose for enjoyment and information. They would learn, through the course of the year, what it is like to live the life of a reader.

If I wasn't sure what the parents had meant by "read," I knew what I meant. I trusted that by the end of the school year all these children would have a love of books and some favorite stories and authors. I hoped they would choose to read when they had time. I expected that they would learn to read for understanding and with purpose, to monitor the message and attempt to self-correct to make sense of their reading. I wanted them to arrive in first grade ready for success. I wanted these children to be readers and to see themselves as readers. Now it was April. My students had taught me that they loved to learn. As a result of this enthusiasm, they had discovered a great deal about literacy. But I wondered if I had accomplished this goal for all twenty-six children in my classroom.

I left the teachers' lounge and headed back to my classroom to prepare for the rest of the day. I had finished my morning as a literacy coach, working with teachers and students at various grade levels. My kindergarten students would arrive after lunch, ready to learn.

As I entered the classroom, I reflected on the changes I had made in adopting a reading workshop approach, which allows students time to become readers. Many of these changes were a result of my experiences with students in my own classroom, but many had also emerged in my conversations with colleagues as I worked in kindergarten through fifth-grade classrooms. I had moved from using guided reading as the only context for reading instruction by discovering a new balance in which it was only one piece of a more flexible instructional framework—from teaching reading to developing readers.

Guided Reading and Guiding Readers

Fountas and Pinnell (1996) suggest that guided reading allows students to develop reading strategies in a socially supported setting as they encounter text at increasing levels of difficulty. Students using similar processes at similar text levels are grouped together for instruction. The teacher begins by offering an introduction to the book that will allow children to read the unfamiliar text successfully and

※ figure 1.1   **Guided Reading.** First-grade teacher Michelle Watts meets with a guided-reading group.

with a minimal amount of work. Then they all read as the teacher works with them, guiding and supporting them. The teacher then identifies a teaching point or two that will be useful to children in their future reading.

For several years, as I taught at various primary grade levels, I used guided reading as, in Fountas and Pinnell's words, the "heart of balanced reading" and observed satisfactory progress in my students. Over time, however, I began to notice that they were not always transferring the strategies they were learning to their independent reading. They seemed to be relying too heavily on my support, looking at me often when they had difficulty. Because of the demands of our schedule, organized so that I could meet with students in small groups, there didn't seem to be enough time beyond guided reading for them to practice what they were learning, a block of time when they were permitted to read independently in a monitored context for an extended period.

As I worked with children, I also began to realize that some didn't need such intensive instruction. Students like Kinsey and Chris, both able to read just about anything they picked up in the classroom, needed more time to read on their own to develop a deeper understanding of the books they selected. Sometimes it seemed that guided reading actually slowed readers down: Jessica, Taylor and Daniel, who had developed good reading strategies, couldn't find books at an appropriate level outside of our guided reading session. Despite their reading abilities, these students rarely chose to read when our work together in a guided reading group was finished. Students like Ryan, who spent most of his time with nonfiction books that were often too difficult for him, didn't have enough opportunities to broaden their reading across other genres.

At the same time, it wasn't easy to support students like Luis, whose second language was English, who needed more experience with language and vocabulary than could be provided in a guided reading group, or Tyler and Mattie, who were not progressing with their peers, and frequently needed more systematic and explicit instruction than was possible in groups with four or five readers. These students often needed stronger book introductions, more supportive prompts, and more focused instruction.

As I thought about my students over the years, I realized that, although they had moved through various reading levels and benchmark books with the support of guided reading, not all had become readers. They might have been able to decode words, tell me the main idea of a story, and retell events, but they had demonstrated difficulty going beyond a literal understanding of the text. They hadn't learned how to choose books, how to talk about books, or how to read for various purposes. I had taught them the strategies they needed to learn to read, showed them how and when it might be helpful to reread, and prompted them to monitor and self-correct. What I hadn't done was help them to develop a reading life.

As I considered my reading instruction at the time, I realized that I was controlling children's reading: I was choosing the books they would read in guided reading. I was determining the books that would be available to them during the limited moments they had to read independently. Class browsing boxes contained books I had chosen. The library housed the books I had selected to put within their reach. Guided reading, not readers, was the center of my reading instruction.

⁑ Another Look at Guided Reading

For me, guided reading begins with Fountas and Pinnell, but I have since found out that it was used as a structure for instruction long before they brought it back to our attention. In *The Foundations of Literacy* (1979), Holdaway defines guided reading as a "form of group instruction in which we introduce children to the techniques of reading new or unseen material for personal satisfaction and understanding" (p. 142). Holdaway suggests that we begin the lesson by taking time to "tune-in" readers, much as we do through the familiar book introduction. He sees what we have come to call a "teaching point" as one of several options after children have read the text to themselves for understanding, and suggests ways to deepen their understanding: by defending a point of view, finding evidence to support their response to the story, talking about strategies that helped them determine meaning, or responding to the story through art or drama.

As I observed the children in my classroom and monitored students' progress across grade levels, I noticed that some struggled to transfer what they learned in guided reading to their independent reading. One day, Lisa Callif, a first-grade teacher in our building, sat down at a table and motioned for me to join her. By the look on her face, I could tell that she had something important on her mind. She let out a long sigh as she searched through her running records. "You have to see this," she said in exasperation as she handed me the most recent text-level assessment for Jacob, which she had just completed. I looked at the running record as she explained.

This was Jacob's second year in first grade, and Lisa was worried. Jacob had managed to appear to be making progress in guided reading groups: He participated in conversations, had figured out some strategies that helped him to read new text, and seemed to be moving forward in his learning. The running record, however, told a different story. Jacob was not using meaning to help him read; in fact, he did not seem to understand that as we read, we try to make sense of the story. His lack of understanding had forced him to rely on visual information, but he did so in an inefficient manner. "It does make sense as I look at it," Lisa said, and plotted out a plan of action to adjust the support she was providing for Jacob. "He has become so used to my introduction in guided reading, he has not been working to make meaning on his own."

I could understand Lisa's concern. I, too, had worked with students who were successful within the context of guided reading but then had difficulty attempting to read independently. As guided reading groups took over my classroom, I wasn't sure that my students were connecting their work in these groups to their own reading life. They didn't seem to be reading, as Holdaway suggests, for "personal satisfaction and understanding."

Students were reading well enough to pass text-level benchmarks, but they were not becoming independent readers. I picked the books. I chose the focus of instruction. I decided the level of support. I asked the questions. I prompted children to go back to the text. I worked through the difficulties of finding something for the other children to do while I met with groups. I planned and prepared literacy centers to support the reading and writing instruction.

I was doing everything. I handed them the book. They were reading. I gave them an introduction to its meaning and located a word or two that might trip them up. They were reading. I jumped in to support them as soon as they were stuck. They were reading. I even chose the teaching point. When they left the group however, they were not reading.

⁘ Considering Readers

I thought carefully about the instruction I was providing in guided reading groups. My classroom community was made up of a diverse population of readers, and it wasn't easy to adapt instruction to each member of a small group. Students at similar reading stages did not have similar strengths and weaknesses, and often required very different support. Small groups were not always the best choice for their learning even though they were easier for management purposes.

Such was the case with Jordan and Shelby. Both were reading early stories with a few lines of text, repetitive language, and pictures that supported the reading. Jordan relied heavily on visual cues and had difficulty considering meaning as she read, ignoring even obvious picture cues. To read successfully, she needed supportive book introductions as well as books for which she had the background knowledge that would help her to read with meaning. Shelby, on the other hand, could pick up repetitive language patterns in the stories she read and did consider meaning. But when she came upon unfamiliar words, she would say anything that made sense, ignoring visual cues. If I wasn't careful during our guided reading groups, Shelby would read large sections of text without monitoring herself or attempting to self-correct.

Both students read similar texts, but they were very different kinds of readers, which made it challenging to support each of them effectively in the same guided reading group. To balance their instruction, I had to look for times throughout the day to meet with them individually: working with Jordan to use meaning instead of relying so heavily on visual information and with Shelby to use the information provided by letters and words to make sure she was getting the message the author intended. To support them both as learners, I had to be systematic yet flexible with their instruction within the classroom and across the day.

Guided Reading: Support for Students or for Teachers?

Before teaching kindergarten and working as a literacy coach, I spent my morning teaching in a first-grade classroom and taught Reading Recovery in the afternoon. I learned a lot from both of these experiences. I worked with many different readers teaching guided reading groups in the classroom, and enjoyed the benefits of one-on-one instruction with struggling readers in Reading Recovery. Both helped me to further my understanding of the many ways in which readers achieve independence. As I gained a generalized picture of reading development, I realized that no two readers learn to read in the same way. I learned what to look for and discovered multiple approaches for offering support. Each time I helped one child over a hurdle I gained tools that were useful with other readers.

Using guided reading in the classroom while teaching students in Reading Recovery helped me see its benefits but also its limitations. There were times when guided reading provided a structure for teaching students new reading strategies, and there were times when it did not. The guided reading format was organized, predictable, and safe, but it didn't always provide the context I needed to be more explicit and systematic with individual children. It allowed me to meet with many students each day, but it didn't provide particular children the experiences they needed to become readers. Reading Recovery lessons helped me to see the power of one-on-one instruction and the progress students could make through focused conversations. Meeting individual needs in the classroom, however, continued to be a challenge.

Time for a Change

During my training year to become a literacy coach, I divided my time between teaching in my own classroom and visiting other classrooms across our district to work with, observe, and learn from colleagues. In classrooms across many grade levels I reflected on students' work and documented their progress while reading and discussing with colleagues the research that supported literacy development. It wasn't long before all this work had me wondering whether I was meeting the needs of all my students, and seeking ways to make adjustments.

Before I could coach other teachers, I knew I had to improve instruction for my students. I began to wonder what was missing in my classroom. Why weren't readers able to transfer their learning to their independent reading? Students needed more time to read, but where would I find it in our busy schedule? I was teaching half-day kindergarten, so there was hardly enough time in our day already. As I worked with small groups and watched students in literacy centers, I found myself more and more troubled by the limited time children actually spent reading. Could I begin by giving children this time to read while I conferred with other students? My colleague Max Brand visited often, and during one of his visits to my classroom I posed this question to him. His only response was, "You want to think about what your kids are getting out of the time in these centers." That wasn't what I wanted to hear. I wanted, "Cathy, do this." I wanted answers! I wanted results! I wanted magic! Honestly, I wanted someone else to solve the problem.

Knowing that the answer was going to have to come from within, I began to reflect more intently on my teaching. This is never fun. When large numbers of students in my classroom are having the same problem, it is usually because I have somehow gone astray in my teaching. I began by asking myself the following questions:

- How much time do I schedule in the day for reading instruction?
- How much time do students spend reading independently?
- Are students engaged during reading instruction?
- Are students able to choose books that are "just right"?
- Are students choosing to read when they have time available?
- Are students reading outside the classroom?
- Do students have favorite genres, books, and authors?
- Do students regularly go to the library to check out books?
- Can students talk about books?
- Who is responsible for the reading work?

As I considered students' work in relation to what I knew about literacy instruction, I realized that I was not using time efficiently throughout the day and that making changes could give students more time to discover what it was like to live a reader's life, to develop strategies to read increasingly challenging texts, and to gain independence. My teaching had become so focused on guided reading that my vision of what was possible had narrowed. Guided reading had provided a structure for reading instruction and had helped me to learn to identify what students needed, but it had not helped students to connect this learning to their reading lives. Because I had begun to rely on it over the years, I had lost sight of the many other opportunities that could support learners in my classroom.

❊ Rethinking Time for Instruction

Although I can teach children some important reading skills and strategies using guided reading, if they are to become readers they also need opportunities to read in other contexts. Children need time to learn about different authors, to read for enjoyment, to choose books that are just right for them, to read in various genres, to make decisions, to learn prereading strategies, to connect what they read to what they know, and to monitor their own understanding. I worry when children are spending large amounts of time in literacy centers so that their teachers can meet with three to five groups of children each day. I worry when teachers talk about children's reading only in text-level numbers. I worry when I ask teachers why children have been grouped together to read and they can't give me a quick answer. I worry when I talk with parents who think the only way their children can possibly become stronger readers is through guided instruction. I worry when administrators base their evaluations of teachers on the number of children they meet with in guided-reading lessons and not on the quality of the instruction they provide. I worry that our vision has become short-sighted.

❊ **figure 1.2** **Student-Led Shared Reading.** Kanna leads a group of readers.

To remedy these problems, I adjusted the structure of the day to allow us to do a different kind of work. I began by reducing the amount of time children spent in centers and providing more time for them to read independently. I introduced a structure that paralleled that of the writing workshop, with which children were already familiar. Each day the workshop begins with a mini-lesson, often a demonstration, a

---

※ figure 1.3   Schedule for Reader's Workshop

Focus Lesson	*5–20 minutes*

Demonstration
- Read-aloud
- Think-aloud

Shared Demonstration
- Interactive read-aloud
- Shared reading

Creation of Models

Independent Practice	*15–45 minutes*

- Independent reading
- Paired reading
- Conferring
- Guided reading
- Small-group work
- Book talks

Share Session	*5–10 minutes*

- To celebrate our reading
- To reflect on our reading and thinking
- To notice details or visual cues
- To reinforce the teaching of the focus lesson
- To extend the teaching of the focus lesson
- To teach something new
- To learn from each other

read-aloud, or shared reading, which helps teach reading strategies and understandings. This mini-lesson shapes the work that the class continues to do independently as I confer with individual students or meet with students in small groups. We close each workshop with a share session to reinforce and extend our learning.

Changing the structure of the classroom day has given me more time to follow children closely and to listen and learn, but most important, it allows me more time to meet children's specific needs. Guided-reading-group time has been reduced; time spent conferring with individuals has been increased. In the past, guided-reading groups didn't always allow me to focus on individual children. Some students, who seemed successful in groups, had learned to compensate for their difficulties and mask their struggles. Other students, who struggled in the small group, were actually reading above the instructional level when

✻ figure 1.4a **Developing Concepts of Print.** Joshua learns to point to the words in his reading as he begins to develop a concept of print. Joshua needs this time to practice this new strategy, which will help him learn to pay attention to print.

✳ **figure 1.4b**   **Reading for Pleasure.** Rachel, Sahithee, and Kristin enjoy poetry together.

working on their own, away from the noise and the interruption of those around them. Because I am more flexible, allow more time to read, and confer often in meetings with individual students, I have a deeper and more accurate understanding of where my students are as readers.

The way guided reading supports the learning in my classroom and in those of the teachers I coach has evolved: It is now one part of a more balanced approach to reading instruction. Not all children need guided reading every day, but they do need flexible support as they practice the new strategies they are learning in a monitored environment. Now students have the time to do the real, purposeful work of a reader.

Now, students read not just the books I hand them but the books they want to read. Kinsey has time to read about how to take care of a cat. Ben and his friends have time to work together to discover all they can about the insects that live in our backyard. Jon has time to reread familiar texts to support the learning he is doing as a reader. If my goal is a classroom of readers, my students need to read. In the sharing environment of our workshop, children begin to talk about books and listen and learn from one another. They learn to read for pleasure, for information, and for solutions to problems. In the workshop, children gain independence.

⸭ Beyond Guided Reading

I am often asked, "How many guided-reading groups do you see in a day?" The truth is, sometimes I see one, sometimes I see two, and on some days I might not see any. It depends upon the needs of my readers. I used to wipe the sweat from my forehead as I entered the lounge at lunch time. Surely, I thought, the more groups I had managed to meet with during the day, the better my teaching had been. Now I've learned to measure the effectiveness of my teaching not by what I have done but by the understanding my students demonstrate. I no longer worry whether all my students are assigned to a guided-reading group every week, because there are many moments during the day for supporting their diverse needs.

I have found other opportunities to encourage readers. During read-alouds and shared reading, for example, I am more intentional about the teaching I do. I use these contexts to demonstrate strategies that will help students think about their reading, finding books and planning language that will support these conversations. I can encourage readers like Luis by taking time to discuss unfamiliar words. I can engage readers like Jordan in conversations that will help her develop comprehension strategies by slowing down during read-alouds and shared reading. I can support readers like Shelby by helping her pay attention to the visual cues in the text during shared reading.

I have broadened my view to take advantage of the many opportunities in a day when I can encourage readers to read for personal satisfaction and understanding while also helping them acquire the skills and strategies they need to tackle increasingly challenging texts. Instead of shaping the children around the day, I shape the day around the children. Guided reading is one of several approaches I use in my classroom to support readers. Unfortunately, in many classrooms, guided reading is mostly about moving kids through reading levels. It has become something we just do. Now, when I take the time to group students together for guided instruction, I make sure it has a legitimate purpose.

In rethinking my teaching, I have also changed the way I plan instruction. Instead of spending countless minutes planning guided-reading lessons for each of three to as many as five groups, preparing literacy centers, and choosing books, I use more of my time for reflection. As I have moved to make the reader the focus of my decision-making, I have worked to find ways to see and document reading progress. Through conversations with other primary teachers making similar changes, I am finding ways to make the work the reader is doing, the understanding the reader is taking from text, more concrete. It hasn't been easy to find ways

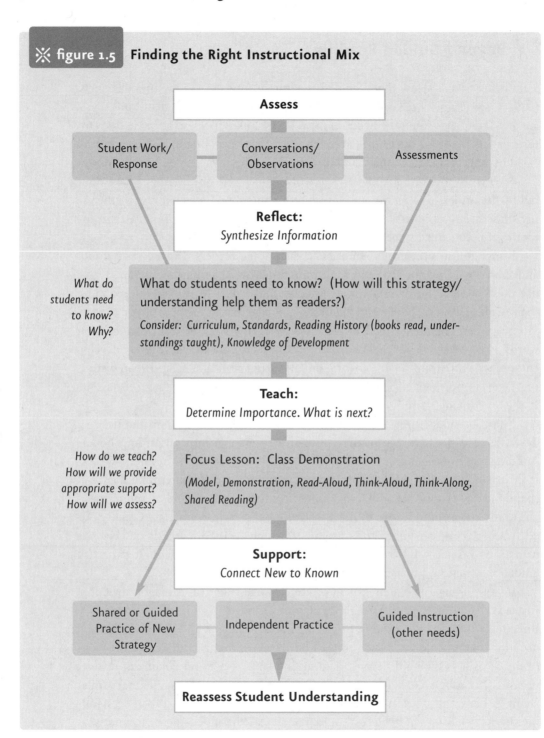

figure 1.5   **Finding the Right Instructional Mix**

Assess

Student Work/ Response   Conversations/ Observations   Assessments

Reflect:
Synthesize Information

What do students need to know? Why?

What do students need to know? (How will this strategy/ understanding help them as readers?)

Consider: Curriculum, Standards, Reading History (books read, under- standings taught), Knowledge of Development

Teach:
Determine Importance. What is next?

How do we teach? How will we provide appropriate support? How will we assess?

Focus Lesson: Class Demonstration

(Model, Demonstration, Read-Aloud, Think-Aloud, Think-Along, Shared Reading)

Support:
Connect New to Known

Shared or Guided Practice of New Strategy   Independent Practice   Guided Instruction (other needs)

Reassess Student Understanding

> ### ✳ figure 1.6   Basics Beyond Guided Reading
>
> - Create a predictable structure for students within the workshop
> - Find extended periods of time for students to read independently each day
> - Organize—and reorganize—the classroom library to support readers
> - Be sure the library includes books of various genres to suit all readers
> - Rearrange the room to make space for quiet reading, small-group work, and collaborative work
> - Help students learn to choose appropriate books
> - Hold children accountable for their reading
> - Find ways to assess student understanding, record observations, and store records
> - Use evidence in student work to make teaching decisions

to document student response and talk about our work developing readers. Drawing on observations about children's reading and writing taken over the course of the day and collected in a notebook, I look closely at my students' work, identifying their strengths and areas of concern, and seeking out patterns so that I can efficiently design instruction that also pays careful attention to students whose progress is slow.

✳ Finding a New Balance

Now, in April, I smile as I look around the classroom. The children are reading. Jon and Trent are rereading Cowley's *Do Not Open This Book*, a favorite from shared reading. Their voices are full of expression as they chime together, "Do not turn the page." Lindsey sits reading quietly by herself, a stack of books in front of her. Ze Fang is reading a new version of *The Three Billy Goats Gruff* that she found in the library. Her familiarity with the story assists her as she reads independently. Colton and Ben are reading about worms, trying to learn the best ways to care for these creatures, which have just arrived for study in our classroom. Brittany and Korall sit with the basket of Joy Cowley books, reading and laughing together. Mahima has a Froggy book by Jonathan London; her knowledge of this character and the similarities between stories support her reading.

✳ figure 1.7   **Friends Share a Book.** Kindergarten students enjoy a book together.

In a primary-level readers' workshop, novice readers learn to make sense of the world of print. Primary-grade children must develop the strategies they will need to learn how words work, to read for understanding, and to make sense of different text structures and genres. Finding the right instructional mix to support such independence is a balancing act between support and expectation, responsibility and practice. There really are no "right" answers, and sometimes that is cause for frustration. We know our kids need to be reading more, but we feel the pressure of other demands on our time. With so much at stake, it is hard to trust the process and hard to trust our children.

According to Marie Clay (1991), "Reading is a message-getting, problem-solving activity which increases in power and flexibility *the more it is practiced*" (p. 6). I want the children in my classroom to spend more time "practicing" reading, to read for a purpose, to understand why we read, and to learn to get themselves ready to read new books. I want to create a supportive classroom environment where novice readers learn how to pick out books that are "just right" for them. In the chapters that follow I will share my search for balance as I have tried to better support primary students in finding their own reading voices.

☼ figure 1.8	Reading Instruction Then and Now

Then	**Now**
Guided Reading as the Center of Instruction	*Reader's Workshop*
• Guided reading for all	• Guided reading as needed
• Teacher-directed	• Student-led/teacher-supported
• Workboard/literacy centers	• Independent reading/conferences
• Teacher knowledgeable about class and development	• Teacher knowledgeable about individual progress as related to development
• Teacher at the center	• Reader at the center
• Time to teach during guided reading	• Time to teach throughout the day
• Teacher as director	• Teacher as inquirer
• Student engaged	• Student engaged and motivated
• Leveled text at the center	• Opportunities to read various genres
• Teacher chooses books at appropriate level	• Child chooses and locates "just right" books

CHAPTER 2

The Focus Lesson: Creating Common Conversations

We need to become architects of classroom cultures that support focus con-versations about reading and provide children with a variety of experiences that draw them back into the world of reading with new skills and better understanding of how texts work.

—Franki Sibberson and Karen Szymusiak, *Beyond Leveled Books*

When I first revised the structure of the classroom day to allow more time for independent reading, I thought that giving children the opportunity to read on their own from books they chose themselves was going to be the catalyst for improvement. I had watched them in guided reading as they learned new strategies and moved through leveled text, but too often they hadn't carried this learning into other reading. I wanted them to apply the strategies they were being taught. As Debbie Miller (2002) reminds us, "Every moment children spend reading independently is a time to apply what they know about words in a real, relevant context" (p. 51).

Even now, when I go into classrooms where most reading instruction happens within the context of guided reading, I am struck by the limited amount of time students actually spend reading. As I work with teachers across grade levels, I see many effective guided-reading lessons, but what is so often missing is the incorporation of new strategies and understandings into children's independent reading. Teachers express concern that their students are not "taking on" new learning, but often guided-reading lessons emphasize a different teaching point each day, and students are seldom given enough time to read appropriate books to make this new learning their own. In a guided-reading classroom, although as much as ninety minutes might be given to reading instruction, children may spend as little as ten to twenty minutes actually reading. That amount of time may be even smaller if students do not participate in a guided-reading lesson on that particular day.

It is true that extended time for reading was important, but to my surprise, that wasn't the greatest benefit of this structural change. What I hadn't really realized when I did most of my teaching in guided reading was that, even though I had been having many different small-group discussions each day, these conversations were often confined to those groups. When I started each reading block with a whole-class mini-lesson that demonstrated new ways to think about reading, used read-alouds and shared reading, and talked together with the whole classroom community about the ways we make sense of reading, I found that these shared experiences helped prepare students for the reading they would do. These conversations not only helped students to begin to learn new ways to approach their reading, they also strengthened our community of readers. Talking together helped us to

- create a common understanding of the way the "work" should look in our classroom
- develop a common language about reading
- talk about the choices we make as readers
- discuss our thinking about our reading
- share the ways we help ourselves when reading is challenging
- experience the work of new authors or new genres in a supportive context
- deepen our understandings about reading over time

Shared conversations gave us a direction to follow, wrapping learning around the literature that filled the shelves of our classroom. These shared understandings gave me ways to talk with the class, and our common experience could be used to anchor further conversations in small groups and conferences. In addition, it gave students ways to talk with each other, not only about the thinking we do or the strategies we use as readers, but also about the choices we make in our reading lives. When the entire community is talking about ways they read for understanding, it becomes less about this strategy at this moment in this book and more about the many ways readers make sense of their reading; less about getting all the words right and more about the things that smart readers do to help themselves. As I observed the benefits of shared conversations, I found ways to make these lessons even more effective.

⁙ Setting the Tone for the Workshop

The conversations during the mini-lesson, or "focus lesson," usually between ten and twenty minutes in length, get students ready for the reading they will do during the workshop. These lessons introduce students to the many possibilities reading offers and the many reasons why we read.

I first saw a mini-lesson called a "focus lesson" in Katie Wood Ray's book, *The Writing Workshop*. Katie was talking about a writer's workshop, but I like to use the term "focus lesson" for the reader's workshop because it reminds me that my teaching needs to be explicit, and my language clear. The lesson has a specific purpose, and that focus will drive much of my instruction. Even here, in this whole-class setting, I can adjust the level of support for students by thinking aloud to demonstrate reading strategies, such as questioning and visualizing, while students think along and try new strategies with me, or using shared reading to try them together.

Students need to understand why we are spending this time, so I usually begin a focus lesson by telling them about something I have noticed or something I think might be helpful for them to know as readers; or I might pose a guiding question

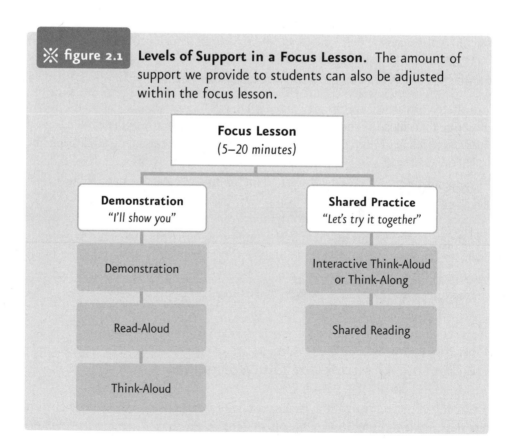

�֎ figure 2.1 **Levels of Support in a Focus Lesson.** The amount of support we provide to students can also be adjusted within the focus lesson.

Focus Lesson
(5–20 minutes)

Demonstration
"I'll show you"

Demonstration

Read-Aloud

Think-Aloud

Shared Practice
"Let's try it together"

Interactive Think-Aloud
or Think-Along

Shared Reading

for them to consider or build on something we have been discussing together. Following this short explanation, I introduce my teaching point, then give a demonstration or set up a shared experience. Finally, I restate the teaching point and send students off to get started with their reading. Mini-lessons should last less than ten minutes. I keep these focus lessons as short as possible, but using books, articles, excerpts from text, and other print materials can add time to the lesson.

⋉ A Look at Poetry

My kindergarten students and I have enjoyed poetry many times, but most of the poems we have shared have either been those I have recited from memory as they learned to join in, or those I have rewritten on large charts for us to read together. Students are not very familiar with poetry books and anthologies, and we haven't really defined a poem in our community. Since they are gaining independence in reading, however, it seems a good time to introduce them to poetry books and a more focused discussion of poems. I have also noticed some stories during writer's workshop that would make great poems. I want to introduce this idea to my student writers as a new possibility, but I know they will need more experience in reading these poems and more focused discussion about poetry before we try to write them.

Today I decide to begin my focus lesson with a guiding question: How are poems different from stories? My hope is that this question will nudge them to connect what they already know about stories to what they will learn about poetry. When beginning a lesson in this way, I am careful to choose a question for discovery to which there is more than one possible answer. As students gather and sit down on the carpet, I tell them, "Many of you have already noticed the new basket sitting beside my chair today." Pulling the basket onto my lap I add, "It is full of poetry books that I thought you might enjoy. I have chosen a few poems to read to you today, and as you listen I want you to think about how poems are different from stories."

Having tabbed a few poems before this lesson, I pull these books from the basket. My class this year has quite a sense of humor, and I know the best way to hook them from the beginning is to read a few funny poems. "Poetry books are collections of many poems," I tell them. "Some are all poems by the same author, and others are collections of poems that are about the same thing." I pull out a few examples and leaf through the pages as I talk briefly about a few collections. "One way poetry books are different from stories is that I can start anywhere in this book. It's a bit like reading informational books. I can choose any poem I want to read, and I don't always have to read from the beginning to the end." I know that I will have a few students who will try to read poetry today, and I make eye contact with these students to make sure they have a sense of how poetry books work.

"I'm going to read a few poems to you. While you listen, see if you can notice a few ways that poetry is different from stories." I read a few poems, and Nada, my rhyming expert, shouts, "They rhyme!"

"What was I thinking?" I wonder to myself. This class also loves a rhyme, and I should have known they would pick up on the rhyming first. "Sometimes poems do rhyme, Nada," I reply with a smile, while reminding myself to be sure that tomorrow's poems don't all rhyme. I like to remember the points we have discussed and often find that by the end of the day, I have forgotten, so I jot "sometimes poems rhyme" (Nada) in my notebook. Sometimes I make a chart of students' responses for further discussion or for added support for readers in the workshop.

"Some books rhyme," Tyler adds matter-of-factly.

"That's true," I say.

The class laughs through the poems. When I close the books to send them off to read, they beg for more. Perfect! "Not today," I tell them with feigned regret, "We'll share a few more tomorrow, but you are welcome to choose a few poetry books from this basket today."

"Nada has told us that sometimes poems rhyme. Did you notice anything else about the ways that poems are different from stories?" There is a silence, but I'm not too worried about whether they did or didn't notice anything at this point. We'll be talking about this in other lessons, and we'll sort it out.

"They're short," Robert tells us.

"They are usually shorter than a story," I agree.

"They're funny," Alonso adds grinning.

"Poems can be funny," I say, knowing that my choices have led him to this assumption. This will be great for later discussion as we read other poems and discover the many reasons people write poetry. "The ones I chose to read to you today were definitely funny! They're like stories in that way, aren't they? Stories can be funny too," I add, still considering Tyler's comment. Already I am rethinking my initial question.

"They're all different," Yakira chimes in.

"Yes, poems, like stories, can be about different things. You guys have me thinking that poems can also be like stories in some ways. Poems and stories are the same in some ways and different in others."

"Today, if you'd like to read some poetry, you are welcome to choose books from this basket," I tell students as they go back to their seats to begin reading from the books they have chosen.

Some students rush to the basket; others move to other reading. I know that some students will immediately consider today's conversation in their reading and that others will need more demonstration, support, and practice before they begin to make these attempts. I don't expect everyone to read poetry today, but I am confident that as I read more poems aloud, as I begin to use a few of the big poetry books for shared reading and put poems on the overhead for us to read together, more students will begin to pick up poetry.

Each day our workshop begins with intentional conversations such as this one, which set the tone for the work students will do, lead children's reading development, and cultivate common understandings in our community. "It is difficult sometimes to understand the significance of a single focus lesson because, in good teaching, the single focus lesson is always a part of a series of lessons and conferences that the teacher is carefully weaving together to build larger, more lasting understandings" (Ray 2001, p. 144). Throughout the year, these shared experiences during the focus lesson help readers to recognize the many reasons we read and develop strategies to read for meaning. As we talk about books, we discuss our reading and learn together. The words that students use to explain their thinking will become the words the entire community will use over and over again throughout the year.

⚹ Choosing Books to Support Conversations

Focus lessons are really quite predictable. If you step into my classroom for a focus lesson, you won't see any magic. No singing—if you're lucky! No dancing—well, not usually. You may be surprised by the simplicity of the teaching. There's nothing fancy about what happens during a focus lesson. You will most likely find me with a book, because focus lessons are, most often, about a book and a conversation.

I'll confess that I used to choose books for the read-aloud somewhat randomly, books I enjoyed, books I thought students would enjoy, or books by our favorite authors. I still choose books students will enjoy and weave our conversations around genres and author studies, but I am more deliberate now. I've learned to choose texts that will support the conversations we're having and offer experiences that will help students connect the stories we read to their lives, to other stories we have read together, or to the ways we make sense of our reading. I now choose books to support my teaching. If I'm talking with students about questioning, I choose books that will make us ask questions. If I'm talking about how to figure out unfamiliar vocabulary using context, I choose texts in which the meaning of words can be inferred.

In Colleen Csiszarik's second-grade class, children were beginning to read chapter books. We both knew that students, many used to reading picture books, would need to learn to use the author's words to create a picture of the story in their minds. We chose to try poetry first because poems are often short; we could encourage children to consider how the author's words and the connections they evoked helped us to create a picture in our minds. Students drew sketches, and then we talked together about our pictures.

However, we really wanted students to use this strategy in their extended reading of chapter books. Once they seemed to understand the basics of visualization, we chose *Marvin K. Redpost: Why Pick on Me?* by Louis Sachar for our focus lessons. We told students that in picture books, illustrations give us a lot of information about a story, but in chapter books we have to create our own pictures using our schema, or prior knowledge, and the author's words. Students sketched in their reading journals as we read the first chapter aloud. Having all students sketch in response to the same text allowed us to compare drawings and the thinking behind them later, when we were discussing the similarities and differences in students' work.

Good books can often improve the effectiveness of a focus lesson. As Regie Routman (2003) reminds us, "If we want readers to be critical thinkers, inquirers, and problem solvers, we need to introduce them to challenging, interesting texts" (p. 118). During my first year as a literacy coach I heard so many questions: "Cathy, do you know a good book I could read aloud to my class that uses a lot of adjectives?" "Cathy, do you know a read-aloud that has a lot of '–at' chunks?" I'll admit that I was puzzled by questions like these. There were so many good books out there and so many more important things to teach students about reading them and understanding them, why would anyone focus so narrowly on skills? Looking back, I realize that this was a necessary step. I like to think that there was already an awareness among teachers that we shouldn't be using worksheets to do all our teaching, that literature would be a much better instruction tool. If students were going to learn to read and write, they should spend their time encountering good literature.

Over the years, as I have worked with teachers, other questions have arisen. Now, as I move down the hall, my colleagues ask: "Cathy, do you have a copy of

Tomie de Paola's *Oliver Button Is a Sissy*? That's the book Debbie Miller used in her lesson on synthesizing information." "Cathy, do you know of a good read-aloud to teach the idea of inferring meaning from context?" I smile to myself at the progress we have made; the subject of our conversations has shifted from drilling on isolated skills to supporting kids in thinking about their reading.

Using the titles that authors of texts on literacy suggest provides a scaffold for us to try as we adjust our teaching, but I have discovered that these books don't always work for me. It seems that the books that work best in my focus lessons are those that I love. If a book is well written it will support almost any conversation in the focus lesson. If I am teaching children how to synthesize information, any well-written book is useful. I advise teachers who want new ideas for teaching reading strategies to gather together a core set of ten to twenty well-written books. These books will anchor conversations and provide common ground for discussion from one lesson to another. It is important to understand the thinking behind the lesson and choose a strong book to support it. (A side note: books that are good for reading conversations also seem to be great mentor texts for writing.)

I have gathered my own small core collection of books I can use for almost any strategy lesson. These are usually titles I enjoy reading and have used successfully with students.

✳ figure 2.2   My Top Ten Focus-Lesson Books

My Brother's a Pain in the Backseat, **Dale Bulla.** This is a book I often use to talk about connections. I have a million connections about riding in the backseat with my two brothers! Many students relate to riding in the backseat with a troublesome sibling.

The Leaving Morning, **Angela Johnson.** Many students have had the experience of moving from one place to another. I've used this book for many conversations: connecting, visualizing, questioning, and inferring. The book itself is short, but there is so much that can be discussed. The words the author uses to help us understand what it is like on the leaving morning create images for the reader: "soupy, misty morning," "pressed our cold lips against the hall window and left cold lips on the pane," and the "bumping noises" as the movers take boxes from one place to another.

Crocodile, Disappearing Dragon, **Jonathan London.** This book is one of my favorites for talking about/questioning. I've used this book with students from kindergarten through second grade, and it always mesmerizes my audience. At the end of our   ▶

discussion we are left with questions that have been answered by the text, those whose answers we need to infer, and some that send us searching for information. This book also works well for talking about the way authors use information to help make their stories more believable. A note included at the back tells more about crocodiles.

Heroes, **Ken Mochizuki.** This book, told in the first person, works best with second- and third-grade audiences for conversations about questioning, inferring, and synthesizing. Students usually have strong feelings about the way Donnie is treated by the other children in the story.

Just Dog, **Hiawyn Oram.** This is another great book for questioning, especially with kindergarten and first-grade audiences.

My Name Is Yoon, **Helen Recorvits.** I have to be honest, I probably like this book just because I think it illustrates some of the challenges second-language learners face as they try to find their place in our communities. Yoon is a strong main character. Questions such as "Why does she want to go back to Korea?" and "Why doesn't she want to write her name?" are not only great for discussion, they also take readers back into the text to find evidence to support their answers.

Scarecrow, **Cynthia Rylant.** This book is perfect for discussing visualizing—the visual images authors create with the words they use.

The Great Gracie Chase, **Cynthia Rylant.** I've had success reading this book with students in kindergarten, first, and second grades. I use it most often to teach students about prediction.

Freedom Summer, **Deborah Wiles.** This book appeals most to second- and third-grade students. A note about the text at the beginning not only gives more information about the story, but also helps to explain where the author got the idea for the book.

The Other Side, **Jacqueline Woodson.** This story about friendship works best with older primary readers; however, even younger readers understand what it is like to try to make a new friend. It also is a good book for talking about the lessons authors try to teach us, how to follow dialogue, and keeping track of characters in a story.

⁚✕⁚ Teaching with Vision: Keeping Our Eyes on the Road Ahead

When I first learned how to drive, I found it difficult to stay between the lines painted on the road. My driving instructor told me that to keep from having to move the steering wheel so much, I would have to stop looking at the road directly in front of me and look instead much farther ahead. Watching the road ahead made it easy to keep the car where it needed to be. Likewise, I have found that observing children and reflecting on what I see informs my planning. My insights help me focus on the road ahead, developing lessons that will connect with young readers as they learn new ways to read for understanding, explore new genres, discover favorite authors, and learn to read with purpose.

As I began to shift my reading program away from guided reading, I'd find myself asking, "What am I going to teach today?" instead of "What do I want students to understand or be able to do after this lesson, two weeks from now, a month from now, or at the end of the year?" I struggled to figure out what my teaching should look like in a focus lesson and far too often found myself teaching something different every day.

⁚✕⁚ **figure 2.3**   **Questions I Ask Myself When Planning a Focus Lesson**

- What do students need to know?
- How will this help them as readers?
- When do we use or consider this strategy or understanding?
- What language will I use to make this strategy or understanding clear to students?
- What books would best support this new learning?
- In what ways does this strategy look different across genres?
- How can I best make this new learning concrete for students (charts, examples, etc.)?
- What evidence will I collect to determine how well students have grasped this idea?

Knowing that I needed to find a way to pay more attention to the "road ahead"—to think about and plan my focus lessons—I began to group my observations of student reading and lessons into categories. In this way, I ensured that different types of focus lessons were not taught in isolation from one another, but woven together across the school year.

Focus Lessons That Teach Students to Live and Work Together in the Workshop

In these focus lessons I begin to establish procedures and develop routines and rituals that will be a part of our reading workshop. I describe the general organization of the workshop and let students know how they are to use their time, where they can read, how they can locate appropriate reading material, and what they are accountable for in reading. Sometimes procedures are the focus of my teaching, but most often this instruction is embedded in my presentation of other concepts. For example, as I show students how to make good book choices, we talk about where they can find these books. As I teach students different ways to think about their reading, I introduce new ways to respond to the story.

During the beginning of the school year when the air is full of the excitement a fresh start brings—new crayons, neatly arranged classroom libraries, the sound of children's voices, and the chance to start anew—our community begins to acquire a rhythm. In these beginning workshop lessons my teaching is usually focused on workshop routines. These first weeks require careful building of rituals and community, thoughtful conversations, and time for us all to get to know one another. This purposeful instruction will help us learn to work together in the workshop.

Although these types of focus lessons occur most often during the first weeks of school, as students settle in, I revisit these lessons as the year progresses. Changes that affect the community will also influence the way children do their work in the classroom. As children become more independent, I try to introduce ways to improve the quality of the work they produce in the workshop.

There are no particular procedures that must be followed in order for a workshop to be successful, but procedures do provide a predictable routine and allow time for me to meet with individual students. It is true that all workshops share some commonalities, but the routines are often determined by the community of learners. My workshop is different from year to year in response to the particular needs of the students in my classroom.

�֎ figure 2.4   Living and Working Together in the Workshop

Focus Lesson: Conversations	Launching: Getting Started	Sustaining: The Road Ahead
The Reader's Workshop	• What does the reader's workshop look like? • What does the reader's workshop sound like?	• What do students do during the focus lesson, independent reading, conference, share session?
Managing Time	• How do readers work during the workshop? • How many books do readers need?	• What does good reading look like? • How do readers manage their time? • What choices can readers make with their time during the workshop?
Managing Books	• Where do readers find books? • How do readers put books away? • Where do readers store books that they are still reading?	• Where do readers find just-right books? • How do we care for books? • How do readers recommend books to a friend?
Working and Talking Together	• How do readers read with a partner? • What does listening look like?	• How do readers turn and talk with a friend? • How do readers talk about books with a friend? • How do we build on a friend's thinking?
Organization/ Accountability	• Where do readers keep a book list? • How do readers record books they have read?	• How do readers record books they reread? • How do readers analyze the book choices they make? • How do readers record the genre of a book? • How do readers set goals for themselves? ▶

※ figure 2.4 (continued)

Focus Lesson: Conversations	Launching: Getting Started	Sustaining: The Road Ahead
Response	• How do readers respond to books? • What should be included in a response (date, title, etc.)? • Where do readers write responses to books?	• What are the different ways readers can respond to their reading? • What are the qualities of a good response? • How do readers support their thinking with evidence from the text?

One afternoon Rachel reminded me of the importance of teaching students about the various aspects of the workshop and their responsibilities during a focus lesson, a conference, or a share session. I sent students off to read and said, "As you are reading, I will be conferring with some students." I didn't think anything about the comment at the time—I'd been talking with students for months—but on this day Rachel looked at me and asked, "What is a conference?" The question nearly knocked me off my feet. I'm a bit embarrassed to admit that as I thought about it, I realized that I really hadn't taught my kindergarten students about conferences. They knew I walked around and talked with students, but I hadn't explained that this was important teaching time. I needed to explain their role in a conference as well as mine. Needless to say, we spent a few days talking about and modeling conferences in focus lessons, and I have since been more careful to explain our activities early on.

Focus Lessons That Teach for Understanding

Most focus lessons in our classroom seem to be about understanding. In *Strategies That Work* (2000), Goudvis and Harvey remind us that "getting readers to think when they read, to develop an awareness of their thinking, and to use strategies that help them comprehend are the primary goals of comprehension instruction." Focus lessons help readers to develop the strategies that will allow them to read for understanding in many genres, strategies such as connecting, visualizing, predicting, questioning, inferring, determining importance, and synthesizing information. During the focus lessons we talk about these strategies and how they help us to read for understanding.

In working on strategies, we've all heard children call out, "I have a connection: My grandma has a red coat too!" We've all seen children struggle to think of a question about a book when they really don't have any questions. Naming the strategies has helped me to talk with students about applying them when they read, but I also want students to understand how they work and why we use them and be able to apply them judiciously. When appropriate, I spend a bit of time introducing each strategy and continue to weave it into our reading conversations throughout the year as we read more demanding texts. My goal is for students to be able to call up these strategies as needed to help them read for understanding.

Reading for understanding is not just a matter of using comprehension strategies. The things we already know about different genres and writing styles can help us when we encounter a new text. Knowing, for example, that most stories have a problem and a solution, or a place where the story changes, or being aware that some stories are cumulative can prepare readers to make sense of what they read. Students need to understand that early leveled texts tend to be listlike: the blue ball, the yellow ball, the green ball. Likewise, knowing how to synthesize the information in photos, charts, and graphs in informational text contributes to understanding. In these lessons, students learn to draw on the features, elements, and structures of various genres to make sense of their reading.

When I walked into Linda Zorich's classroom, I discovered I was just in time. Linda, a second-grade teacher, was sitting in her rocking chair, and her students were gathered at her feet. Each student had a reader's response notebook in hand and a pencil. All were waiting expectantly for Linda to begin. Linda's class had been studying books by Tomie de Paola and talking about characters. Many of her second-grade students were beginning to read chapter books and needed help learning to follow characters from chapter to chapter. Linda also felt that they needed to understand how we learn about characters from events in the story and infer character traits from their actions.

Linda had chosen *Oliver Button Is a Sissy* by Tomie de Paola for today's lesson. A piece of chart paper hanging from her chalkboard was divided into two columns, one entitled "Description," the other, "How do we know?" Before Linda began to read, she reminded students that they would be describing Oliver Button throughout the story and using events from the story to support their inferences. Then she began to read, talking with students along the way to fill in the chart and think about Oliver. Because this was not the first time students had read this story, they easily stopped along the way to discuss the character. The final chart looked like this:

Description	How do we know?
sissy	• didn't like to do what boys like to do • picks flowers • likes to jump rope • plays with paper dolls • likes to dress up • likes to dance
hard worker	• practices at dance school • practices routine • proves he can do it
embarrassed	• the boys wrote "Oliver Button is a sissy"
independent	• keeps doing things even when he gets teased
performer	• talent contest
talented	• danced
brave	• only boy in the dance class

※ **figure 2.5** **Focus-Lesson Conversations: The Language of Learning**

Language for Learning

Reading for Understanding	Launching:	Extending:
	• We preview books to get ready to read. • We read to understand the author's message. • We decide what is important as we read. • We notice when we don't understand.	• We use different strategies to make sense of our reading. • We read different genres in different ways. • We reread when we are confused. • We slow down when we're having a hard time understanding. • We ask questions when we are confused.

✳ figure 2.5 (continued)

Connecting	Launching:	Extending:

Connecting

Launching:
- We make connections between books and our lives to help us to think about the story.
- We make connections between books we've read.
- We make connections between books and the world.
- We use what we already know to help learn new information.
- We have more connections with some books than others.
- The more connections we have to the reading, the easier it is to understand.
- Pictures can help us make connections.

Extending:
- We make connections with characters, setting, and events in the story.
- We connect characters, themes, and events in similar books.
- We connect the work of authors across books.
- We connect the work of different authors.
- We use our connections to help us predict what will happen in a story.
- Our connections help us create mental images.
- We use our connections to make inferences about characters, themes, and events in a story.
- We use what we already know to help us to synthesize new information.

Predicting

Launching:
- We predict to get ready to read.
- We use the title to predict what the story will be about.
- We use the picture on the cover to predict what the story will be about.
- We make predictions as we read.
- We predict each time we turn the page (new chapter).
- We predict to figure out new words.

Extending:
- Connections help us to predict and understand.
- Sometimes our predictions are correct, and sometimes they are not.
- We use evidence from the text to guide our predictions.
- Questions guide our predictions.
- We use the table of contents to think about what information we may find in a nonfiction book.
- We use headings to think about what a section might be about.

▶

※ **figure 2.5 (continued)**

Questioning	Launching:	Extending:

Questioning

Launching:
- We ask questions to better understand our reading.
- We ask questions when the reading gets confusing.
- We ask questions to help us to monitor our reading.
- We ask questions to know more.
- We use our connections to help us ask meaningful questions.
- We ask questions before, during, and after reading.

Extending:
- We ask more questions when we don't have a lot of schema for our reading.
- There are questions that move us forward (predicting), questions that pull us back (monitoring), and questions that really make us think (inferring).
- Some questions are answered directly by the text.
- Some questions are not directly answered by the text so we have to infer the answers to our questions or find information in other sources.
- We ask questions to determine what is important in our reading.
- We ask questions to help us to synthesize new information.

Visualizing

Launching:
- We create pictures in our mind as we read.
- The illustrations can have an effect on our mental image.
- We use our schema to help picture the story.
- The author's words help us to visualize the story.
- Readers picture the characters, setting, and events of a story.
- Visualizing keeps us interested in the story.

Extending:
- Readers create unique mental images.
- The picture in our mind can change as the author tells us more (synthesis).
- We use the author's words to help create mental images when reading informational texts.
- We use mental images to help connect what we already know to new learning in informational text.
- We infer meaning as we create pictures in our mind.
- Creating a picture in our mind can help us to understand new words.

✳ figure 2.5 (continued)

Inferring	Launching:	Extending:
	• Some questions are not directly answered in the text, and we must infer an answer. • We infer before, during, and after our reading.	• We use what we know and the clues the author gives us to infer meaning. • We use what we know and the clues the author gives us to figure out the meaning of unfamiliar words. • We infer a character's feelings based on actions in the text and our own experience. • We infer a character's intentions in determining why characters make particular decisions. • We infer the theme of books.
Determining Importance	Launching:	Extending:
	• We determine important details in the text we read. • Chapter titles and headings can help us determine what is important.	• The conventions of informational text help us determine importance. • We determine important events and details when we retell a story. • We can highlight and record important information to remember.
Synthesizing	Launching	Extending
	• Our thinking changes as the author tells us more. • We combine our schema with the information the author gives us.	• We synthesize information to determine the main idea of our reading. • We can compare books we have read or authors we have studied.
Genre Study	Launching:	Extending:
	• What is the genre of this book? • When do we read this genre?	• What are the characteristics of the genre? • What are the features, structures, or elements of this genre? • How is this genre similar to/different from other genres we have studied? • How do we use comprehension strategies to make sense of this genre?

Focus Lessons That Provide Strategies for Independence

At times primary-grade students may need alternative strategies for helping them-selves when their reading is challenging. These strategies might include using pic-ture cues, considering context, searching for further visual information, rereading, reading on, monitoring, and self-correcting. Primary-grade students need to learn about words *as* they learn to read for understanding, to decode *as* they learn to make sense of their reading. Although these strategies are often the focus of con-versations in our small groups, individual conferences, or during other parts of our day, such as word study and writer's workshop, there are times when these discus-sions need to be the subject of focus lessons.

Reading fluency encourages understanding, and understanding creates fluen-cy. The way a child reads dialogue—using vocal expression, pauses, and changes in pace—may demonstrate how much that child understands about a passage. We do not teach reading as a performance skill, however, and rarely ask experienced pri-mary readers to read aloud. Fluency can also help younger readers encountering a new text. When students read word by word, they can find it difficult to think about the story; fluent reading allows students to use meaning to help when the text is challenging.

Early in the year, I teach beginning kindergarten readers to read by pointing to the words with their finger. This helps them pay attention to be sure the words they use their finger to be sure the words they say are the words they see. As students begin to demonstrate a 1:1 match between speech and print, start monitoring their reading, and correct their own misreading, they are ready to let their eyes take over this important work. Beginning readers, who have been taught to read using their finger, may need to be taught to read using their eyes.

Even though most students usually quit pointing to words as they read, I noticed that many were still reading word by word, making it hard for them to think about the story because the pace of their reading was so choppy. I wanted them to understand that we read as if we were talking. To illustrate, I wrote some of the words from *Wishy-Washy Day* by Joy Cowley, a story we had read several times in shared reading, on a transparency and cut them apart.

As students gathered on the carpet to read a big book for a focus lesson I told them, "I have noticed as I have been listening that some of you are reading word by word." I demonstrated by talking in a choppy rhythm, isolating each word. "When we read," I said, "we say the words together, just as if we are simply talking. That helps us to hear and think about the story. Let me show you." Some students do better with a visual example, so I moved to the overhead, placing words together in phrases the way I would read them. I read the sentence. We continued with a few more sentences, but now trying the reading together.

Moving back to the big book I read the text word by word and then the way we had practiced together. "See the difference?" I asked. "Let's try it together."

✳ figure 2.6	Focus-Lesson Conversations: Strategies for Independence
	Ways Smart Readers Help Themselves
Using Picture Cues	Pictures can help us figure out tricky words and make sense of the story.
Balancing Cues	Readers make sure their reading makes sense and looks right.
Rereading	Readers go back and read when they are stuck: • Beginning reader: to beginning of page • Developing reader: to beginning of sentence • Experienced reader: to preceding word or two Readers reread for different reasons: • When they come to a tricky word • When they don't understand • To check their reading • To self-correct.
Attending to Visual Information	Readers try something that looks right: • Beginning reader: attends to beginning letter • Developing reader: groups first three to four letters, searches through the word, checks the end • Experienced reader: takes apart complex words efficiently
Monitoring and Self-Correcting	Readers notice when their reading doesn't make sense or look right and try to fix it.
Try It and Read On	When the reading is tricky, smart readers try something. *(I have students try something instead of skipping the word. I have found it helps them to use the structure of the sentence to hear what might sound right, and often the first attempt is correct.)*

Focus Lessons That Help Students Develop a Reading Life

When guided reading was the context for teaching reading in my classroom, I must admit that developing a reading life was the most neglected aspect of my teaching. I didn't really think about how important these conversations were for students who didn't come to school with a lot of experience with books. Talking about our choices and decisions as readers isn't always considered curriculum. In Ohio, however, state standards require students to read independently for various purposes and have reasons for choosing their independent reading materials.

As adult readers, there are things we know about developing a reading life that these young apprentices can learn as active members of the learning community. Taking my kindergarteners to the library for our school bookfair is always an exciting time (once they get over the fact that they can't check out books because the library is closed for the sale). One year, as the children spread out on the floor,

---

✷ figure 2.7   Focus-Lesson Conversations: Developing a Reading Life

	Launching: Getting Started	*Sustaining: The Road Ahead*
Book Choice	What books do you like to read? • Readers choose books on topics that are interesting to them. • Readers choose books by favorite authors. • Readers read about favorite characters. • Readers read books their friends have recommended. • Readers read books from favorite series.	• What are the reasons readers choose different books? • Where do readers find out about new books (friends, reviews, book lists, library displays, etc.)? • How do we balance the types of reading we are doing? • Are we reading books from various genres? • Are we balancing the difficulty of the reading we are doing? • What features and information do readers use to choose books (information, picture, chapter, etc.)?

※ figure 2.7 (continued)

	Launching: Getting Started	Sustaining: The Road Ahead
Knowing Yourself as a Reader	What types of lists do readers keep? • Readers keep lists of books they have read. • Readers keep lists of books they want to read.	• How would you describe yourself as a reader? • What are your strengths as a reader? • What do you need to do to improve in your reading? • What do you like to read? • What goals do you have as a reader?
Talking About Books with Friends	• How do we talk to a friend about a book we think they'll like?	• How do we recommend books to a friend? • How do we confer with a friend? • How do we participate in a book-talk?
Reading Choices	• Where do readers read? • When do readers read?	• What choices will help make us better readers? • When do readers abandon a book? • When should readers stick with a book?
Reading Purposes	• Why do readers read?	• Why do readers read more than one book at a time?

pulling books off the shelves and carefully turning through the pages, one of the parent volunteers commented that my students always take such time with their book choices. I consider this quite a compliment and a reflection of the conversations about books we have had all year.

One of my favorite focus lessons for starting this conversation is to have students bring in their favorite reading from home. This not only provides information for our discussion and background knowledge about their reading lives, it also helps me to see if my classroom library contains everything this community of readers will need. This focus lesson usually carries over for a couple of days because I bring in books that I am reading first, before I ask students to bring in their books. It is interesting to see how the books students choose change with age. Kindergarten students tend to bring in books that have been read to them over and over since they were little. Older readers tend to bring in other reading materials: magazines, comics, informational text, and functional reading.

✳ Cultivating Lessons Over Time

On two recent occasions I have had the distinct pleasure of listening to Lester Laminack, author of *Saturday and Teacakes*, talk with teachers. In his conversation, which weaves gently through life stories and points to ponder, he has consistently mentioned the importance of the fact that writers *notice* all that happens in the world. He's not the only writer I've heard say this. The difference between writers and the rest of us isn't so much that they notice, but that they write about what has caught their attention and then play with their observation to make sense of it. Teachers are also close observers. Moving through our classrooms, we take the time to note what students understand and to consider what may be just within their reach. We watch and we record our observations, looking for patterns that will inform our teaching and help us to shape lessons over the following days and weeks.

✳ Growing the Seeds of Our Teaching: A Closer Look

To get a glimpse of lessons over time, let's take a closer look at a few over several weeks of teaching to see how they develop. I include three snippets from a series of lessons intended to help students read increasingly demanding text. (Many lessons have taken place between each of these lessons, and more will follow.) These community conversations are guided by the underlying question students seek to answer: What do smart readers do to help themselves?

Plant a Seed

In beginning lessons I plant a "seed" to raise awareness of a new strategy or concept I think will be helpful for students to know. I demonstrate this new idea, sometimes thinking aloud to show how it can be applied.

My kindergarteners and I had been reading books by Mem Fox, and—Mem would have been pleased—the children loved her stories. We laughed together through the *Magic Hat*, smiled together as we read *Koala Lou*, and were surprised together by the sad ending of *Tough Boris*. I had noticed that students, perhaps in an effort to pay more attention to words, were not always using the obvious clues provided by the pictures and the content of the stories they were reading. Students needed to better balance meaning with visual information. For this lesson I had selected Mem Fox's book, *Where Is the Green Sheep?* This short book would allow me to make my point quickly, laying the groundwork for future conversations. Knowing how much the children had loved this author's writing, I was sure they would enjoy this story and that many would be able to reread it later independently. Our focus lesson would demonstrate the importance of making sure that reading makes sense; an obvious point, but necessary.

With the students seated comfortably on the carpet, and twenty-six pairs of eyes waiting expectantly to hear another story by this favorite author, I began reading *Where Is the Green Sheep?* using beginning visual cues, but making sure that my reading made little sense. It didn't take long for the students to realize that their beloved Mem Fox would never subject them to such garbage. By page three of the story, the students were clearly frustrated, and I was almost worried that Mem Fox herself would walk in and hear me torturing her writing. The mumble became a roar as students exclaimed that the reading didn't make any sense. After conceding that they were right, I told them, "That's what I have been noticing about your reading. You have learned so much about letters and words that sometimes you forget to think about what would make sense. Our reading always has to make sense." I vowed to begin again and make sure that my reading made sense.

The children loved the story. They laughed all the way through it, and I smiled to myself, knowing that Mem would have been thrilled by their reaction to her story. We talked about the importance of making sure that we read the author's writing the way the author intended it to be read, being certain that it makes sense. "Today as you read I want you to make sure that what you are reading makes sense. If you notice that it does not, then go back and try to fix it," I told them before sending them off to get started, knowing that some students would begin to consider this today in their reading, and that for others it would take many continuing conversations.

Grow the Idea

During shared reading, in conferences, and in small-group teaching, we further our conversation. During these lessons I demonstrate how smart readers monitor their reading using textual meaning and visual information. I pay attention to opportunities to praise students when they notice their reading isn't quite right and note changes in students' responses. I overhear partners reading: "That doesn't make sense," Robert tells Tyler as they read *The Little Snowman* by Lynette Evans. Brittany pauses as she attempts an unfamiliar word by substituting one that starts with the same letter but realizes that it doesn't make sense in the story. It is time to *grow the idea* in our reading community by helping students discover ways to help themselves as readers. Sometimes this means bringing to their attention strategies that other students are discovering or demonstrating new strategies that might be helpful. During these lessons we will talk together about a strategy or idea and learn to use it, transferring the accountability from teacher to students.

Readers do many things to help themselves when their reading doesn't make sense. Since this group has not been balancing meaning with visual cues, I decide to teach them to reread to get back into the story. I have also noticed that Kristin is one student who does this automatically. I use the big book *The Hungry Giant* by Joy Cowley for this lesson, since it is most like the type of reading students are already trying to do in the classroom. Preparing for the lesson, I take sticky notes and cover a few words in the story I think students might have to pause to think about. Students have enough knowledge about the beginning sounds of words that I could leave the first letter visible, but I decide to cover the entire word. I really want this group to predict what would make sense; then I'll show the first letter to help us to figure it out.

"I have been listening to you read, and I'm so happy to begin to hear you stopping when your reading doesn't make sense. I've noticed that sometimes it's hard for you to fix your reading once you've noticed something isn't quite right." Heads nod as I continue, "Today I'm going to show you something I think will help you. Kristin reminded me of this yesterday when she read with me. Kristin goes back and rereads when she is stuck." Kristin smiles broadly, and a few students shout, "I do that too!"

"Sometimes when I'm reading and I notice something isn't quite right, or if I can't figure something out, I can go back and read the words again. This really helps me to think. Let me show you." I demonstrate by stopping at the sticky note, rereading, and trying a word that would make sense. Then I uncover the actual word, showing the beginning letter first and then the rest of the word to make sure I'm right. We continue to read the story, rereading at the sticky notes, and making meaningful attempts to figure out a word when we are stumped. Students are surprised by the long words they figure out before they've even seen the letters. "Our brains are pretty smart," I tell them. When we have finished the story I send students off to begin their own reading. "Remember today, when you notice something that doesn't make sense, go back and reread like Kristin does."

Try It

In lessons that follow we talk about rereading, discussing how far back we go to reread and how many times we might have to reread. Students begin to *try it* while I monitor, support, and guide them as needed. "I am so proud of all of you," I say to them one afternoon. "You are working to make sure that your reading makes sense and looks right. You've found lots of ways to help yourself as you try to fix your reading. Today as you're reading, I want you to put a sticky note on a place where you noticed something wasn't quite right and you found a way to fix it. We'll share some of your smart thinking at the end of our reading."

At this point we have worked together to try new ways to correct our reading when we notice something doesn't quite make sense. Students begin to tell me some of the other ways they have used. (This can sometimes become a bit daunting because students think they need to share everything they have thought and figured out on their own.) We begin to record students' discoveries of other ways to self-correct when a text is challenging. These conversations will continue as the texts they read become more difficult. I will look for evidence of new understanding in conferences and across conversations.

Supporting Independent Work in the Focus Lesson

The focus lesson shapes the work that will continue in the workshop. Lucy Calkins (2001) describes the "architecture of a minilesson": it includes connection, teaching, active student involvement, and a link to ongoing work. Kathy Collins (2004) calls this "teaching directly into the children's independent reading" (p. 18). The conferences and small-group instruction that take place after the focus lesson will often reflect the conversation at the beginning of the workshop. Students consider this new learning in their independent reading, and then as the community comes back together, it becomes the impetus of the discussion that pulls the workshop together.

Michelle Watts, a first-grade teacher, sits at the front of the carpet area in her classroom. A partially completed chart containing nonfiction conventions hangs on the wall beside her. This is one of the first lessons of nonfiction, and Michelle wants her students to understand how some of the features of this genre can help them to make sense of their reading. "We've been talking about nonfiction conventions," Michelle reminds the class as she reviews those that have already been discussed: photographs, labels, and captions. Continuing a conversation that has been developing for days, Michelle asks, "How do they help us when we read?"

"It's easier to see what they're talking about," Ian responds.

✳ **figure 2.8**

Creating Models During a Focus Lesson. First-grade teacher Michelle Watts adds to a chart of non-fiction conventions during a focus lesson.

"They tell you more," Kiersten adds.

"Today," she continues, "we're going to learn about the maps you can find in books. I went to the library and got a bunch of different map books for you to look at today. Some books are all about maps and other books use maps to tell you more." She adds the word *map* to the class chart. Then she reaches beside her and pulls out *Map It*, a big book full of maps, and turns to the table of contents. "How does the table of contents help us?" she inquires, referring to a previous conversation.

Carlee raises her hand. "It helps you know what page you can learn on."

Michelle looks thoughtful for a moment, "I'd like to learn about landforms." She studies the table of contents carefully.

Students near the front, trying to assist their struggling teacher by pointing and reading aloud, instruct Michelle on where she should look for maps about landforms. She turns to the suggested page, pausing to notice a few different types of maps along the way. Finally she finds the map about landforms and together they talk about what they notice. The class takes a moment to discuss the map key as well as the photographs, drawings, and labels that help them to learn about landforms, but today's lesson isn't about reading maps; that, Michelle informs me, will come later this week in social studies. Her goal today is to help students become familiar with the different types of maps in books and how these maps can help them as readers. While presenting new possibilities for their reading, she helps to make these informational texts more accessible to these young readers.

"Some books are *about* maps, and some books *use* maps to help you see what they are talking about," Michelle reminds the class. "Today as you read, I want you to look for maps in books. If you find a great map, something you'd like to remember, or a map you'd like to share, you can get paper here to write about it." This wandering phase is a chance for Michelle's students to discover more about maps in books. It is also an opportunity for her to listen and assess what they already understand, and to determine what would be helpful for them to know next.

Some students go directly to the new basket of map books Michelle has brought with her today. Other students meander over to the informational sections of their classroom library and begin looking through baskets labeled "United States," "countries," "Time for Kids," and "space." Students in this classroom obviously know their library well, quickly finding baskets that might contain books with maps. "I'm reading about my state," Fernanda tells a friend as she picks a book about Mexico from the "country" basket.

A student who has been out of the room during the focus lesson returns and is quickly intercepted by Carlee and Brooke. "We're finding maps in books," Carlee reports. "And we're drawing them," Brooke adds matter-of-factly. Everyone goes back to work.

Mustafa holds a state atlas that is nearly as big as he is. "Where is Ohio?" I hear him mutter to himself. "O-H-I-O," he says, looking through the table of contents. "There it is," he exclaims, pointing, "page 76."

Students work around the room, by themselves and in pairs, at their tables and on the carpet. A large world atlas rests between Josh and Jared. Looking at a map of the world, they are both drawing their own version. "That's water," Joshua tells Jared as he takes his pencil and colors in the space where the ocean would be. It isn't long before a conversation begins and the pencil is replaced by a blue crayon. Jared has taken the time to draw many of the state boundaries within North America on his map, labeling Ohio and Texas even though they are not labeled on the map he is using as a guide.

Students continue to read and draw maps until the end of the workshop while Michelle confers with individual students about what they have found. Finally, students come together in a circle on the carpet to share the books and maps they have discovered: books with maps of bedrooms, states, countries, and journeys. Michelle talks with students about the many maps they have brought to the circle. As students talk, referring often to the labels they have noticed, Michelle sees an opportunity to extend her teaching, helping students begin to see the way these labels guide readers' thinking about the map.

Creating a Reading Community

Despite hectic schedules our family manages most evenings to sit down together at the dinner table. As sports, school demands, and social calendars try to creep into our lives, we still sit down as a family in the evening. This time allows us to talk about all that is going on in our worlds. In the classroom, focus lessons are much the same. Despite hectic schedules and all the demands on our time, my students and I need to find time each day to gather together and talk about our reading lives. These conversations not only create a culture of readers, they also help support the work readers do each day in our workshop. I'm still working to make focus lessons more effective, but there are a few points I try not to compromise. I've found these "rules" to be important to the success of my focus lessons:

- Fit in a focus lesson each day
- Connect yesterday's lesson to today's teaching
- Watch the time and stick to the point
- Tell students what they need to know; don't make them guess
- Have students turn and talk to each other; make sure all voices have a chance to be heard
- Draw out quiet students
- Consider individual needs in conversations
- Base focus lessons on students' needs
- Don't analyze a book to death
- Enjoy!

CHAPTER 3

Independence Through Conferences

One afternoon during reader's workshop, I knelt down beside Katie to talk about the book she had chosen to read, *The Big Kick* by Beverley Randell. Even though I had read this story aloud a million times, I was having a hard time understanding her retelling. She didn't quite seem to get the gist of what she was reading. The story is about Tom and his dad who, while out in the yard playing soccer, kick the ball over the fence and have to try to find it. Since Katie seemed to be having a hard time understanding the story, I wanted to try to determine what was making the reading challenging for her. Was she actually having trouble reading the story or just difficulty understanding it? I asked if she would read a page or two to me and took a running record as she read.

As I listened, I noticed that when she got to an unknown word she would stop and look at me. My prompts to "try it" produced only puzzled looks. She was uncertain about how to help herself. I thought that if I gave her some strategies to try, she might be able to read with more success. Unfortunately, because Katie was not attempting to read tricky words at all, I had little information to go on. Was she able to use meaning to help figure out unknown words? Was she using available picture cues? Was she looking at the word and thinking about what it might be? There was no way for me to know the cues she was attending to.

As I talked with Katie I said, "I notice that when you are reading and you come to a word you don't know, you stop and look at me. I want you to try to figure out the word on your own. Let me show you something I think might help. When you are stuck, go back a little and reread; then, when you reach that hard word, try something that makes sense. You can use the picture and think about the story to help as well."

We practiced rereading and attempting to figure out the word when she was stuck. Then, since she was still having difficulty, I reread with her and let her try the word, lowering my voice as hers took over. We did this several times, with occasional prompts from me. I praised these attempts, even though she did not always produce the word in the text, because they did allow me to see what information Katie was using to read new text. I put her back on my schedule for the following day. I wanted to follow up quickly, to make attempting an unknown word something she does independently.

✳ Conferences That Shape Independence

While focus lessons allow me to develop common conversations in our classroom community, conferences allow me to shape my instruction to individual students. Changing my schedule to allow time for conferences has not only helped me to carry focus-lesson conversations into the workshop and learn about my students as readers, it has also allowed me to address specific student needs.

The readers in our primary-level classrooms read at their own pace and often have different needs. Instead of working with Katie in a small group, where my attention is divided, in a conference I can focus on her, jumping in quickly when she needs support, prompting her responses as necessary, and praising her attempts at reading. My goal is to support Katie with what is next in her learning, helping her to use new strategies to read increasingly challenging text with understanding.

Having time within the day to meet individually with students has made it easier for me to address the specific needs of my students. In classes of twenty-five or more, students are often not in the same place at the same time. Not everyone is going to be reading a book that is good for asking questions when my focus lesson is about that strategy, not everyone is going to need to learn strategies for figuring out challenging vocabulary, not everyone is going to need to learn to check through a word (search visually), and not everyone is going to need help in monitoring their reading. Conferences allow me to tailor my instruction.

- *Guided Conferences:* I teach students something they need to know about reading and we try it together. I am there to provide immediate support.
- *Conferences That Support the Teaching of the Focus Lesson:* I follow up on my teaching of a new strategy or understanding from the focus lesson.
- *Conferences That Extend the Teaching of the Focus Lesson:* I am able to teach something that builds on the focus lesson and extends student learning.
- *Conferences That Develop the Reader:* In these conferences, often more conversational, I help students to develop a reading life.

■ *Assessment Conferences:* I am able to find out what the child knows and understands about reading.

⚜ Readers Who Benefit from Individual Instruction

In a classroom full of children, instruction for the whole class, or even small-group instruction, does not always meet everyone's needs. Students from novice to fluent reader can vary significantly in their reading expertise. When I relied on guided reading, I could not always listen carefully to individual children and observe them without interruption. I now collect information about students throughout the day, but I gain the most insight in reading conferences. As I confer with each child, I monitor where that child is developmentally as a reader. By listening, observing, and taking careful notes I can determine what children know and understand about reading, and what they need to know next.

In making independent readers, teaching decisions play an important role. Guided reading required common ground for all the readers in the group. Conferences, in contrast, provide an opportunity to learn about the reader, but they also make it possible to teach each child in keeping with what that reader needs to learn next. In a one-on-one teaching situation, problems can be mediated quickly with appropriate demonstration, explicit language during instruction, time to practice, and genuine praise. By carefully observing children's reading behaviors and making informed decisions, I am better able to help them make continued progress.

The number of conferences I schedule each day depends on the issue, the amount of time available, and the needs of my students. I meet more often with students who may not be making the progress of their peers. I may also meet with some readers for several days in a row until they have control of the new strategy or understanding. For some readers, a conference is essential in their development as a reader. They seem to make greater gains with short one-on-one conversations tailored to their needs.

Readers Who Need Specific Support: Marcie

Marcie was a beginning reader. She participated in large-group discussions and enjoyed read-alouds. While listening to stories she could make connections to the text, predict what would happen, answer and ask questions related to the book, and demonstrate her understanding in discussions, illustrations, and drama activities. In writing, she could develop an idea and could write using a core of known words that she could read. She could say words slowly, accurately recording the beginning and ending sound, and attempting middle sounds as well.

Marcie read familiar books with ease, but she was having difficulty reading new stories. My running records indicated that she was not using visual information effectively or paying attention to more than the beginning letter of words as she read new text. Since her strength was in using meaning to support her reading, I felt that getting Marcie to use visual information would help her to read more challenging texts independently. The information I collected told me that she should be able to handle this task.

I decided to put Marcie in a group with four other children who were having the same difficulties. My plan was to meet with this group for a few days to demonstrate and practice, using the meaning of the story and the first two or three letters to help read new text. I expected Marcie to be able to take on this new strategy quickly because she showed every sign of being ready to use it.

Although she was probably the strongest reader, she fell apart in the small group: She did not use the same thinking strategies she used during read-alouds even when she had books that should have been appropriate for her, nor did she use the information she already knew about letters, sounds, and words. Even after working with her group on this strategy, she showed no sign of using it. I was stumped.

I knew I needed to work closely with Marcie and decided to meet with her individually in a conference to attempt to figure out the problem. Happily, in a one-on-one setting, Marcie quickly picked up the new strategy. She liked the immediate support and reinforcement I could offer as she began to attempt this strategy on her own. Having me beside her seemed to give her the confidence she needed to try something unfamiliar. I really did nothing more than provide a bit of demonstration and encouragement; she soon understood what she needed to do and was ready to practice this new strategy on her own.

Many young readers reach a point where they need the support of an experienced reader to learn to use new information, but determining the appropriate amount of support to offer is a balancing act. Too much can become cumbersome, slow down the process, and take away independence. Not enough leaves children struggling. I try to be flexible in my thinking and planning. In Marcie's case, this meant finding the right context, providing explicit language and demonstration, scheduling individual time to prompt and reinforce her attempts as she gained control of this new strategy, and then being sure that she had the appropriate books so she could continue to practice on her own.

Quiet Readers: Tori

Shy and quiet, Tori didn't like to talk during focus lessons, and the other students in small groups seemed to talk right over her. Throughout the year she made steady progress, but she seemed to demonstrate the most growth as a result of conferences. She needed individual attention to gain confidence and learn to be flexible in her use of reading strategies. During conferences I could monitor her progress, provide the appropriate amount of support, and demonstrate new strategies that would help her.

Readers Whose Second Language Is English: Billy

Billy's family spoke Spanish at home. When he entered kindergarten he loved to participate, but it was very difficult to understand him because he used a Spanish-English mix of vocabulary and some words I'm sure didn't belong to either language. Later he would mumble through a sentence, but he sometimes inserted simple nouns that gave me a clue to the topic of his conversation.

Although Billy's speech was difficult to understand, he showed signs that he made sense of much of our talk in the classroom. He followed directions, would react enthusiastically to stories read aloud, and demonstrated rapid understanding of math concepts. Billy learned sight words quickly as well, and it wasn't long before he had mastered the basic concepts of print.

Billy's difficulty in his reading was vocabulary. While he could read early leveled text, he did not have enough experience with English to know much of the vocabulary in books. The introductions he required before reading were more detailed than those required by his peers. He needed time to activate his prior knowledge and connect stories to his experience. He needed discussion that tapped into the vocabulary of the story. I also found it helpful to choose books that focused on similar themes, for example, books about school, for several meetings before moving on to another topic.

Meeting with Billy in a conference was the best way to continue to be systematic in my instruction. It allowed me to introduce him to new concepts, as well as to tie his book to other books I would provide for him to read independently. It allowed me to keep my language simple and respond to his questions and comments without worrying about the input from other students that sometimes took conversations off track.

Struggling Readers: Emily

Emily, a second-grade reader, was not making the same progress as her peers. She had been working to close the gap since kindergarten, but learning to read had not been easy for her. In many ways it seemed that the gap had only grown wider. During a visit to her classroom, I watched her in a guided reading lesson. I couldn't figure out why she was there; the book the group was reading was far too difficult for her. She spent most of her time looking at the other children and trying to figure out what she should do. I could only imagine what she was thinking.

Her teacher informed me that Emily didn't fit into any current group, but since she needed to meet with Emily every day, she had put her in the lowest group. I wondered if ten minutes in this group was really better for Emily than ten minutes of reading books at her own level independently or receiving a few minutes of individual instruction in a conference.

In my classroom I often meet in a conference with children who are significantly behind their peers. Most often these readers are working on short books that can be read quickly. These readers also benefit from reading a familiar text, which they can do during a short conference. These meetings also allow me to keep my focus on a particular teaching point over several days until the child begins to demonstrate understanding.

Readers Making Good Progress: Ben

Ben was an avid reader of nonfiction. He loved to read to learn and inspired those around him to do the same. I checked in with Ben periodically, but his conversations in the classroom and his responses to reading helped me to know that he was making good progress. During the year I conferred with Ben to help him to work on fluency and understand unfamiliar formats in nonfiction, and occasionally to encourage him to balance his reading, but our conversations were usually short. He was able to understand focus lessons, often without additional support. He could talk with other children about books and demonstrate his understanding in a variety of ways. It wasn't necessary to meet with him as often as with others, since the focus lesson usually supported his reading, and I could observe evidence of growth throughout the day.

✖ The Structure of a Conference

During independent reading, I move around the room as children read, talking with some about the books they have chosen, hearing from others about the stories they are reading, checking to see if they are reading for understanding, and providing support. In teaching children in a reading workshop, I consider conferences the most daunting yet most interesting part. Conferences are sometimes unpredictable, but I have found ways to structure them to work effectively. In the beginning of each conference I sit down beside the child and listen to the child talk about his or her reading. Then, considering the information I have just gathered as well as the child's history, I decide the teaching move that would be most helpful. Finally, I talk with the student and teach something that will help in the future.

Listen

In conferences I learn more than what the child knows about reading; I learn about the child as a reader. During the first part of the conference my role is to listen

✖ figure 3.1   **Conference.** Michelle listens as Joshua, a first-grade student, talks about his reading.

carefully, to gather and record information, and to ask questions or respond. In talking one-on-one with each child I learn about what is easy and what is difficult. I learn about the books each child likes to read and favorite authors. I can determine if a child can pick books that are just right for continued progress. I learn about the areas in which the child is confident as a reader and about the challenges that make the child uneasy.

In the beginning of a conference I listen. As I move around the room I ask questions: "What are you reading?" "Why did you choose that book?" "Tell me about the story." These are questions I would ask of any reader. They help me to understand, they build a picture of the reader, and they tell the reader I am interested in what they are reading. This information will help me later. I show interest and enthusiasm and make sure I understand what they are telling me. The message remains the focus of the reading and our conversation.

My conversations in conferences focus on the individual reader, but I also gather information by talking about books the child is currently reading. I consider what I have learned in one conference in relation to what I already know about the reader's history. I try to stay focused on the big picture. Although I go into a conference with a good deal of background knowledge about the child, I always pay attention. I may think I know what the child needs next, but careful listening may indicate that a different direction would be better. The unpredictability of a conference is at times intimidating, yet it is this flexibility that makes it an effective context for encouraging independence.

✳ figure 3.2   Thinking Through Conferring

As I listen and confer with students, I consider these questions:

- Did the child understand the story?
- What comprehension strategies does the child use, or need to know, to understand this text?
- Is the child balancing meaning, structure, and visual information when reading?
- Is there evidence that the child is monitoring during reading?
- Is the child self-correcting or attempting to self-correct errors?
- Is the child's reading phrased and/or fluent?
- What is the child beginning to do that might be the focus of the next conference? Is this information consistent with other observations of this child?

When I meet with novice readers or readers who may not seem to have a complete understanding of the text, I often ask them to read some of the text out loud for me. I want to be sure that the book they have chosen is an appropriate one. If the child is having a hard time understanding the story I can determine whether the difficulties arise from decoding or from comprehension.

Reflect

After I have listened to and talked with a child, I consider not just this conversation but all I know about the child. I ask myself, "How is this child making sense of the reading?" It is this question that will help to frame my thinking as I identify my teaching point. My goal is for students to understand what they are reading; if they don't, I ask myself, "What is getting in the way?" When I notice a breakdown in understanding, I try to figure out why the child is having difficulty.

I think about past conversations and consider any patterns I see to determine the best instruction for this child. I choose a teaching point that will help in other reading, not just in getting through this book. What language will support the child? What opportunities for practice will support the child? What structures will best support the child? Is this something I am seeing in other students in the classroom? Designing instruction around the reader means quicker progress. One conference does not make a reader, but many conferences over time support growth toward independence.

It is easy to respond to the reading in a conference, but what I really want to do is to respond to the *reader*. To this end, I consider all I know about this reader,

---

⁂ figure 3.3   What Is Making the Reading Difficult?

- Is the book too challenging?
- Does the child have enough background knowledge (schema) for this particular book? Is the child having difficulty figuring out unknown words?
- Does the child know what to expect in this genre, author, or story structure?
- What comprehension strategies might be helpful with this text; is the child using any of them?
- Is the child having difficulty with unfamiliar vocabulary? Is the child adequately monitoring the reading?

all the information I have gathered about this child throughout our time together: the child's history as a reader, my running records, the child's interests, the type of learner the child is, the kinds of challenges the child can handle, any other observations and conversations. I think about where this student needs to be going as a reader and what lies ahead.

Teach

After all this, I teach, or better yet, I talk. I talk with readers about what I have noticed and what they need to consider next. I talk about what I have heard, possibly about what I have experienced, possibly about what I think they should try. I talk—and I listen—focusing on the new strategy or idea that is needed next. Many times I demonstrate this new thinking, give a name to something they are doing, or link our discussion to other learning we have done together as a class. My goal is always to teach for independence. For this reason, I try to keep my teaching point on the edge of a child's learning by choosing a generative point; something the child can use to approach many texts, not just this one book, this one sentence, or this one word.

Because it is easy to see two or three or more teaching points that would be helpful, this is where I am always careful to step back for a minute, take a deep breath, and choose the one most helpful to this child. I make my point, and I make my exit.

Teaching the Reader: A Closer Look

I have been working in this third-grade classroom for a few days now, but I still like to take a few minutes after the focus lesson to watch as students settle in to their work. As I watch, I notice Justin. He's reading his book one minute and flipping pages the next. Looking again I realize that he is at the beginning of the story, and thinking about it I realize that he was at the beginning yesterday and the day before that. I am also reasonably certain that this isn't the same story.

Walking over to Justin, who is seated comfortably on the floor, I settle in beside him. "What are you reading?"

"*The Boring Room*," Justin replies, having misread the title.

"This looks like a good book," I say, trying to start some conversation. "Do you mind if I take a look?" He hands me the book, Fleischman's *The Borning Room*, and

I glance through the pages. This isn't the first time I have found myself beside Justin for reading. We spent time together during his second-grade year as he tried to make progress. He's come a long way, but I doubt that he is quite ready for this book. "Do you like it?" I ask. Justin looks at me and shrugs his shoulders, "It's all right."

"I'm wondering what made you choose it," I say, digging deeper, hoping to get to the heart of this issue. Justin shrugs his shoulders again, "I looked at the cover," he says, not so convincingly. Glancing at the cover, I'm not sure why it would even have caught his attention. I'm thinking it's quite possible that it was the closest book he could grab.

"Did you read the summary on the back?" Justin tells me that he did not, with a look that makes me think it may never have occurred to him to do so. I realize that he may need some help picking out books. "How do you usually choose books?" Justin shrugs again. I glance through his reading log for this week and see that my suspicion is correct. He was reading something different yesterday, and the day before that. I decide to talk with him about choosing books.

"Justin, when I'm choosing a book I usually do just what you did. First, I look at the cover. If the title looks like something I might be interested in or the cover catches my attention, I then read the summary to find out more about the story. Sometimes I look at the chapter titles or read the beginning too. Let me read this summary to you," I tell him, and start to read. As I watch his face it becomes obvious that this wasn't the story he thought it was. "Are you still interested in this story?" "Nah," he responds, shaking his head.

Talking with Justin, I discover that he has had a difficult time choosing books for some time and would be willing to allow me to help him find a book he might be interested in reading. He is obviously struggling to find his reading niche. As we talk, he can't really tell me anything he has read lately that he likes, but he does begin to share some of his interests. I listen carefully and move through the room gathering a few books I think might work.

"These might be interesting to you," I tell him, handing him a fistful of chapter books. I grab the first book and read the title and summary. "Will you take a look at these other books? Read the title and summary like we just did to see if any of them seem like stories you'd really like to read. I'll be back." Having already spent a good deal of time talking with Justin, I decide to leave to let him read through the summaries. I'll keep an eye on him as I continue with conferences and return right at the end to see if he has found something he likes.

I used to think that there was a magical conference, some perfect combination of words that would keep readers moving forward. I tried to find the perfect teaching point for every child in every situation. It was as if I thought I would finally say something so profound, further instruction in reading would never again be required. I got over it. I have walked away from conferences amazed at how well they went, or wondering why my thinking was off, and sometimes simply to think more about a student before making any teaching decision. There is no guarantee that I will always make the right move or provide the ideal words of advice. I try to remember that it is the power of these conferences over time that will make a difference.

It is a bit like the Crazy Horse Monument being created near Rapid City, South Dakota, not far from Mount Rushmore. Looking at the unfinished monument now, it is easy to tell that the image being carved into the rock is Crazy Horse. Each blast gives it more shape and brings it closer to completion. All of them together will finish this masterpiece.

CHAPTER 4

Book Selection: Less Leveling, More Focused Choice

There is nothing I like more than meeting someone who has read a book I have read. I love the conversation as we hash over surprising twists, annoying characters, fascinating lines, creative plots, as well as amazing—and disappointing—endings. There is nothing I like more than having someone hand me a book they think I will enjoy. I listen carefully to the readers in my life and their conversations about books. I love meandering into the school office to find our secretary, Anna Deri, an avid reader, discussing the book she is reading with a passing teacher. I love it when Lisa Potts, my friend and colleague, rushes into my office to say, "Cath, you have *got* to read this." Like the children in my classroom, I am still a student of reading.

School taught me to read, but I didn't become a reader until much later, and I still often have to work at it. I really don't know how I learned to read; it just seemed that one day I could read anything I picked up. I'm going to date myself now, but I remember "reading" in first grade. I don't recall the teacher ever reading to us, but I do remember *Dick and Jane.* We sat in long rows with the teacher at her desk in the front of the room. We would open our books, all of us at the same time, and read chorally. I think we read the same book over and over for that year, although my hunch is that we read more than one version. "Look, Dick. See Spot run. Run, Spot. Run." always seemed to be the same story even if the book had a different cover.

In second grade Dick and Jane were placed in a closet. Our class was the first to get *Signposts*, a basal reader. It was a huge book, quite cumbersome, and full of stories or parts of stories. I was placed in a group with four other students, and amazingly I never changed groups. Apparently my reading really never got any better or any worse in comparison with the other children. When I finished the fifth grade, I was still reading with that group.

All through elementary school, reading instruction followed the same predictable routine. We'd gather at the reading table while the other students completed seatwork or maybe read through the colored tabs of the SRA box. We'd turn to our selection and take turns reading out loud while other students followed along with their eyes. I used to sit at the table with the other four children, figure out what I would have to read, and read it while they were reading their parts to be sure that I knew all the words. I'd then zone out until the person beside me was reading, find the spot, and be ready when the teacher looked at me. Afterwards we might answer a few questions the teacher, or more likely the manual, asked about the story, and then we would move back to our seats. Other than venturing down the hall to the library one day each week to check out a book, we were never given time to read self-selected books, and a magazine in the classroom would have been seen as a serious offense. Many of us learned to read but did not become readers.

If I learned to read at school, I learned to value reading at home. Thank goodness my mom was a reader. She was such a reader that my brother and I used to sit in the hall and peek around the corner as she settled into her book. We'd wait until she was comfortably arranged on the couch. After a while she became completely absorbed in the story, and then we'd saunter casually into the room to ask her if we could do something that at any other time she most likely would not have allowed. We learned quickly that she'd say yes to just about anything when she was reading, since she was so caught up in her story. We had books around the house growing up, our local library was just a bike ride away, and there wasn't anything better than receiving new books from a school book order.

Still, as I reached middle school I had a hard time finding books I enjoyed reading, and by high school I only read what had been assigned to me. It seemed too difficult to build a reading life—reading enough on my own to find favorite genres or authors—and keep up with all the assigned readings. We never had conversations about what other students my age were reading, so I was never able to use the knowledge and experience of others to help me through times when I couldn't find my next book. We were never given time in a classroom to read independently, and no teacher ever handed me an unassigned text saying, "Read this. I think you'll like it."

If we are not careful with guided reading, our classrooms could look much like the classrooms of days gone by: a steady diet of basal stories replaced by a steady diet of leveled text. Our students could spend more time keeping busy than actually developing their own lives as readers. Leveled texts can, at times, be a useful tool for instruction, but they aren't always well written or engaging. Students need to have time and choice, not only to learn to read but to want to read.

My job is to help students fall in love with books. I am not naïve enough to believe that my words alone will make them readers, but I am certain that the words of their peers and of the authors whose books surround them in the classroom will entice them to come back for more. My students need stories that sink deep inside, that become part of their ears, their minds, and their hearts. They need stories they can hear over and over, stories they can look at over and over, and stories they want to read over and over. The students in my classroom are students of reading, but they need more than reading instruction to become readers. I have to provide them with the very conditions that have hooked me as a reader: good books and engaging conversations.

❖ Introducing Possibilities

Recently I heard Shelley Harwayne tell a group of fifth-grade students that they needed to write every day in order to capture their childhood. Maybe reading is the opposite. Perhaps writing helps us to look back, while reading moves us forward. Supporting students as they become readers may help them to envision their future even as it offers them a way to learn about their world. If students are going to become independent readers, I want to help them discover what readers do. Some students already know about the reading life; having been read to since the day they were born—sometimes before—they move easily into the routines of the reading workshop and are quickly engaged in the life of books. Others, however, need to be taught not just reading but how to live in the world as a reader.

The first thing I do is to encourage students to want to spend time reading. I have found books to be the greatest hook on this journey. In my classroom, and across grade levels, I talk about authors I know students will love; authors like Jan Brett, Eric Carle, Mem Fox, Angela Johnson, Jonathan London, Cynthia Rylant, and Jane Yolen, who have written a large collection of books that students will want to return to for their own reading. In addition to picture books, for more transitional readers, I introduce books by authors who are widely published or who have developed series books: Dan Greenburg, Mary Pope Osborne, Ron Roy, and Louis Sachar.

During her second-grade year, my daughter Cassidy was fortunate to have a teacher who valued reading. She read aloud to the class every day. The books she introduced often pushed Cassie to find other titles by the same author or other parts of the same series. When her teacher read *Wayside School Is Falling Down* by Louis Sachar, we had to make an emergency run to the public library so that she could check out a copy to read ahead of the teacher. She couldn't wait to find out what was going to happen next. Each night she would read the next day's chapter, walking into the classroom the following morning a step ahead of her friends. Her teacher was good at choosing books the kids would enjoy and reading them well. Cassie encountered many new writers that year and discovered more options for her own reading.

One way to hook students on reading is to read books they can relate to, books in which characters have experiences similar to their own. Both *Lilly's Purple Plastic Purse* by Kevin Henkes and *My Name Is Yoon* by Helen Recorvits are stories about finding our place in our school communities. We've all dealt with bullies like those in *Stand Tall Molly Lou Melon* by Patty Lovell and *The Recess Queen* by Alexis O'Neill. Besides stories of school and friends, students also enjoy stories of family. A few favorites in our classroom each year are *The Pain and the Great One* by Judy Blume, *I Love You the Purplest* by Barbara M. Joosse, and *Koala Lou* by Mem Fox.

Using trade books for read-alouds in focus lessons and during shared reading not only creates common experiences within the community but introduces students to books they may wish to visit again. I bring in trade books that have always been a hit with students: *Up, Up, Down* by Robert Munsch, *Bugs!* by David T. Greenberg, *Giant Steps* by Elizabeth Loredo, and *My Little Sister Ate One Hare* by Bill Grossman for younger readers. Older primary students seem to enjoy books with interesting plots: *The Remembering Stone* by Barbara Timberlake Russell or *The Stranger* by Chris Van Allsburg. These readers are also interested in chapter books, poems from anthologies, and articles from magazines, such as *Sports Illustrated for Kids*.

※ **figure 4.1a**

Our Favorites. Each week we vote on a favorite book from the week and place it in the basket. Students love to return to these books over and over again.

List of Favorites. These are some of the books that Karen VanVleet's kindergarten students have voted as their favorites during this school year.

❊ Characteristics of Books That Can Support Readers

"That's all well and good," one might say, "but I want my students encountering books that help them learn to read." Let's face it. One of our greatest struggles in primary-level classrooms is getting kids to read books that challenge them at the appropriate level. Many students want to read books that are too difficult for them. Emergent readers are easily attracted to books with detailed illustrations in which pictures tell the story. Even sticking a piece of candy on early leveled books wouldn't be enough motivation for some of these readers to find them appealing. In the higher grades, where transitional readers grow in numbers and more chapter books and series books begin to circulate, novice readers are eager to jump on the bandwagon and read only chapter books. Without some good conversation they will ignore the books that would be more suitable for their learning.

All too often our response to problems of appropriate book choice is to fill baskets with leveled books for readers or to choose books for children that *we* deem as "just right." I have found that, in addition to teaching through conversations across the year, teaching ways to look at books to determine if they are just right is also helpful. Every classroom should contain a wide variety of books for a range of readers. We need to look beyond leveled texts at trade books, which even novice readers can return to and successfully read, in whole or in part, again and again. Many of the characteristics I consider in choosing books for guided instruction can also be useful in finding books to support readers' progress. Sibberson and Szymusiak (2001) define "supports" as "those text elements that can be used by readers to build or clarify understanding" (p. 17).

For guided reading I think about the layout of the text, the language and structure of the story, the amount of additional information in the illustrations, and my students' background knowledge. In helping readers to make good book choices for themselves, I stress the same characteristics. I also point out books that use repetitive language, which can make them easier for novice readers: *Click, Clack, Moo: Cows That Type* by Doreen Cronin; *Guess What?* and *The Magic Hat* by Mem Fox; and *Would You Rather* by John Burningham all use repetitive words and phrases.

In addition, books with very little text and strong picture support encourage students to read independently: *No, David* by David Shannon; *A Beastie Story* by Bill Martin, Jr.; and *Where Is the Green Sheep?* by Mem Fox are examples. I try to choose books that young students are likely to be able to read by themselves once they have heard them read aloud: *Yo! Yes?* by Chris Raschka; *From Head to Toe* by Eric Carle; *Go Away, Big Green Monster* by Ed Emberley; and *Carlo Likes Reading* by Jessica Spanyol.

Books that draw on students' prior knowledge, books with favorite characters, and books by familiar authors can also be easier for students to read and understand. The connections students can make between a current book and their own experience or between a new title and other books they have read can also offer support for their reading. My kindergarten students easily relate to the problems of David, the main character in some of David Shannon's books, who seems unable to stay out of trouble. Other favorite characters whose experiences recall their own are Jonathan London's Froggy, Joy Cowley's Mrs. Wishy-Washy, Helen Lester's Tacky the Penguin, Louis Sachar's Marvin K. Redpost, Anne Mazer's Abby Hayes, and Megan McDonald's Judy Moody. Reading one book in a series can also provoke enough interest to send readers to other books in the same series.

⁂ figure 4.2

Buddy Basket. Our media specialist, Liz Deskins, suggested that I make a basket of books for buddies to read together. In our kindergarten classroom we decided to use books from shared reading. Placing two copies of each title in bags allowed students to find a friend and enjoy familiar reading.

Challenging books can be made accessible to students through repeated readings, shared reading, and listening centers. Sometimes the help of a friend is enough. In our classroom, favorite parts of texts are reproduced on posters illustrated by students and hung on the walls. My students love the ending of Paul Galdone's *The Three Billy Goats Gruff*: "Snip, snap, snout. This tale's told out." They love to reread the repeated verse in Nikola-Lisa's *Shake Dem Halloween Bones*: "Shake, shake, shake dem bones now. Shake, shake, shake dem bones now at the hip hop Halloween ball."

Readers: The Heart of Reading Instruction

As I round the corner of the kindergarten hall toward the rooms full of our new first graders, I can barely contain my excitement. In my hand I hold a book I am sure is perfect for Zach. It is the latest title by Jane Yolen, *How Do Dinosaurs Get Well Soon?*, which shouted Zach's name from the shelf as I browsed through the children's section of our local bookstore. My anticipation grows as I near his classroom and look inside to see if it is a good time to sneak in and show him my latest find. I am certain he will be thrilled that Jane Yolen has written another book about dinosaurs.

Zach had been in my classroom as a kindergarten student. An artist from the day he walked in the door, he loved to draw detailed pictures of dinosaurs, name them, and fill me with more dino-facts than I needed to know. At the beginning of the year it was a challenge to get him to spend time with books because he wanted to spend it all drawing. From our conversations it was clear that Zach enjoyed nonfiction topics, and I used those to hook him. With the help of nonfiction I was gradually able to get him to increase the amount of time he spent reading.

As time passed, however, I knew Zach needed to balance his nonfiction reading with fiction, and dinosaurs came to the rescue. As I began to read dinosaur fiction to the class, he joined us in making sense of the stories. By the end of the year, Zach's favorite fiction still included dinosaurs, but his interests had widened to include other topics, such as bugs and animals. He still spent much of his time with nonfiction, but he was beginning to choose some fiction titles. I felt confident that he was well on his way to becoming a reader.

Passing the office, I finally arrive at Zach's classroom. I step inside, greet a few old students, who seem surprised to see me, and move swiftly to Zach, standing near his desk close to the door. "Mrs. Mere?" he says, as if he can't believe his eyes. The smile on his face widens.

"Zach, I am so happy to see you," I say, as a few kids gather nearby to see what I'm holding in my hand. "You will not believe what I found at the bookstore. Jane Yolen has written another book about dinosaurs! I thought of you when I saw it," I say, putting the book in his hands. Zach's eyes light up as he looks at the new story. "I brought it today for you to read. I knew you'd be excited. Keep the book in your classroom to read and enjoy, and I'll come back in a few days to hear what you think about it." Suddenly Zach's smile fades and he hands the book back to me. He pauses for a moment and gets a serious look on his face, "Mrs. Mere, you'd better take the book with you. I just don't have time to read in here." My heart sinks as I glance around the room. The white worksheet in the middle of Zach's desk seems to be waiting for him to get started.

No time to read? In first grade? I knew Zach's words were not entirely true. His teacher did read aloud to the class each day, and students did meet with her in guided reading groups, but as I looked around the room, I saw only a wooden book display case that held books related to the theme they were discussing. The rest of the classroom library was shelved spines out above the coat rack. Students couldn't see the covers of these books, couldn't touch these books, couldn't read them and discover the authors' words.

All the conversations Zach and I had during the previous year, all the gains Zach had made as a reader, didn't seem to matter in this classroom. He would probably continue to learn to read and decode words during this first-grade year, but would he discover wonderful new nonfiction or fiction? Would he have conversations with his teacher and his friends about books they just couldn't live without? I doubted it.

Our classrooms say a lot about us. After placing guided reading at the center of the school day for so many years, I finally realized that I needed to make major changes. I wanted my students to keep reading at home and as they moved along in their own out-of-school lives, to become readers living a reading life.

Monitored Independent Reading

In *What Really Matters for Struggling Readers*, Richard Allington (2001) tells us, "If I were required to select a single aspect of the instructional environment to change, my first choice would be creating a schedule that supported dramatically increased quantities of reading during the school day" (p. 24). As he reminds us, studies have found that "tasks completed with high rates of success were linked to greater learning and improved student attitudes toward the subject matter being learned" (p. 44). In other words, students need to spend time reading, of course, but reading books that are just right for them.

Adding independent reading time isn't enough. Many of the conversations in my classroom throughout the year, in focus lessons and in conferences, are intended to guide students in choosing appropriate books independently.

"I want to read this one," Torii pleaded to Abby, as I walked by. Abby was adamant. "We should read this one," she announced firmly. I was surprised to hear the two of them arguing about which book to read. We had talked often about the give-and-take of reading with a partner and had even role-played possible solutions to this very situation. We had words to help us when our friends wanted to read their book first: "We'll read yours first, and then we can read mine." We knew the words to use to compromise: "Let's find another book we both want to read." These two students were usually able to get along well with everyone, and both understood the art of compromise. Why were they having so much trouble together? I moved in to see if they would be able to work this out.

When it became apparent that a solution was not forthcoming, I inquired, "What is the problem?" as I sat down beside the two of them. "I want to read this book, and Abby won't read it with me," Torii said in exasperation. Normally, Abby would have said something like "We'll read yours first," so I was a bit surprised; it was unlike her to refuse so firmly to cooperate. "Abby, why don't you want to read Torii's book?" I was curious to hear her answer. "It's not a just-right book for us," she said matter-of-factly. I had to smile. Abby was absolutely right; the book had detailed illustrations, but it was not one that the two of them would be able to read.

Abby was one of the first students to understand what a "just-right" book really was. She could easily determine whether books were a good match for her or not and made great gains as a reader because she spent so much time reading successfully. Throughout the year I had tried to figure out how Abby could so easily regulate her own learning and, from that, to find ways to show the other students what she so easily understood. Students like Abby helped me develop conversations about making good book choices.

⋇ Curriculum for Making Choices

Primary students like Abby can handle more responsibility on the road to independence than we often allow them. When guided reading was the context for most of the reading instruction in my classroom, I chose the books. In the reading workshop I realized that, although students still needed to spend time reading books that were a good match, I also needed to find ways to teach them to choose these books on their own. For me, that meant spending time teaching kids to do for themselves what I had been doing for them. It meant finding ways to explain the work that readers do in choosing appropriate books. It meant changing my classroom library to better accommodate the diverse learners in our classroom community. It meant reading aloud often to introduce new possibilities. It meant talking about books to create a common language that would shape our conversations across the year.

Children are often taught that if they can't read five words on a page, they need to find a new book. But choosing an appropriate book goes beyond a five-finger rule, especially in classrooms where readers range from emergent to transitional, and early to fluent. The rule does not work for children reading picture books or leveled text with fewer than five lines on a page and is rarely a good indicator for chapter books when the issue isn't readability, but comprehension. If I can keep students focused on understanding—which is, after all, why we read—talking about just-right books becomes an easier task.

One of my greatest challenges has been discovering ways to help my students learn to make good book choices. Making good choices is difficult, and not a skill that children know automatically. That is not surprising, since in the primary grades children's ability to read more challenging texts is constantly changing, and the books available vary widely in difficulty, content, and length. The way an emergent reader chooses books that are just right is different from the way a transitional reader makes book choices. A few guiding questions can be helpful. These questions ask students to think hard about why book choice is important in becoming a reader. Here are some of the questions that frame our discussions across the year:

- What is a just-right book?
- Where can readers locate just-right books in this classroom?
- Why is it important to spend time with just-right books?
- How do readers balance their reading?
- Are the same books just right for everyone?

❉ figure 4.3 Choosing Just-Right Books

Focus Lessons Across the Year

Launching:
- What are just-right books?
- What are easy books?
- What are challenging books?
- Where can we find just-right books?
- How do we record the difficulty of our book choices?
- How much time should we spend reading just-right books?

Extending:
- Why do we need to read just-right books?
- How do we analyze our book choices?

Conference Starters

- Tell me about what you have been reading.
- Let's look at your reading log.
- I notice you've been reading a lot of _____. Tell me about it.
- What books have you been reading that are just right for you?
- Where have you found just-right books?

As students grow and change in their abilities, as units of study change, and as new books enter the library, we revisit the subject.

❉ Focus Lessons Developed Over Time: Book Choice

In my kindergarten classroom we spent the first months of school discovering that books told a story and learning to use the pictures to help us understand the story. We learned to talk together about books. Through conversations in these early days, students began to acquire the language of books. In focus lessons, we followed the story by bringing the pictures together with our words, connecting events with *first*, *then*, *next*, and *finally*. Reading with a partner, we practiced placing the book between us and taking turns talking about the story: "I tell about a page, then you tell about a page." I listened to students talk together and noticed them begin to transition from telling about the pictures as separate events to weaving them into stories. At the same time, we were also learning about print. During these early days students read familiar stories. Gradually we began to add stories that were not familiar, stories that contained only a small amount of text, which was highly supported by the pictures.

Even though my kindergarten students were beginning to be able to read some early stories, they were spending most of their time with picture books that would be considered challenging instead of balancing their reading time with easy and just-right books. They were still reading many of the familiar books that we had shared together earlier in the year, but they were not attempting to read new books. Clearly, they needed help to grow as readers.

Most often as I work across grade levels, I set out to define "just-right" first, but it just didn't seem like the right plan this particular year. Before this group of students could locate "just-right" books, we needed to define "easy books" and learn why it was important for beginning readers to spend time reading these books. Repeated readings of familiar books help novice readers to notice the features of print, discover new details in the illustrations, develop strategies for reading, improve fluency, and gain a deeper understanding of the story.

Easy Books

Students began each day reading familiar books from the browsing baskets on each table. I knew we could use these examples to begin our conversation. Each student also had a browsing bag of books he or she enjoyed reading and rereading. Baskets of easy books, with short lines of repetitive text supported by the pictures, were within reach.

First we needed to define "easy." Over many days we talked about activities that were easy for us to do and compared these activities with our reading, developing a chart to help us to find easy books. Robert told us it was easy to throw a ball. Nada thought it was easy to sleep (I couldn't argue with that!). Sandra got quite a laugh when she announced that it was easy to crash when she was riding her bike.

Using books from our familiar reading to support our conversations during several focus lessons, we talked about what easy books were and how they helped us to become better readers. Students realized that some books are easy the first time they read them, but most often these are books they have read before. We agreed that we could easily understand easy books and that we could usually read them quickly.

During conferences I began to ask students about the easy books they were reading and help them to articulate what they were noticing about books. I could account for what students I had conferred with that day were reading, but I found it difficult to monitor the book choices of the entire class. To help me in

figure 4.4 **Easy Books.** Students wrote about something that was easy for them to do. We used these examples to connect to finding easy books in our classroom.

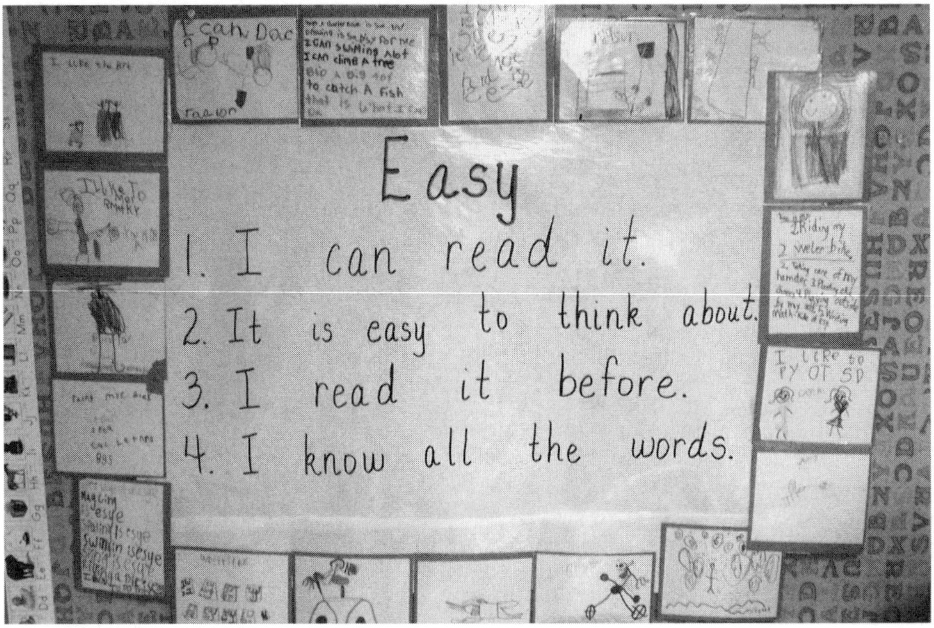

assessment, I asked them to write down the titles of the easy books they had read each day. This way I could quickly see what kind of reading students were doing. As I looked over these lists, which most children, surprisingly, liked making, and conferred with students, I realized that most of the easy books they were reading were from their browsing bags.

I wanted students to know about other easy books, besides the ones in their bags. During our next focus lesson I said, "I have been looking at the lists you have made of the easy books you have read, and I have been very impressed. I can't believe how much reading you have been doing, but I've noticed that most of the books you are reading come from your browsing bags. There are other places in the classroom where you might find books that are easy for you to read. For example, the baskets on your table at the beginning of each day contain many books that you have read before and that are easy. Today, while you are reading, I'd like you to really look for some easy books and be ready to share them. Remember to write down the titles as you read today."

After the focus lesson I watched students to see if they were beginning the search for easy books. Then I met with students, keeping the conferences focused on locating and reading easy books. "Tell me about what you are reading. Is this an easy book? How do you know?" As we came together at the end of the workshop, we shared easy books and places they could be found in our classroom. Teaching students to choose easy books took much longer than I had expected, but while they were learning to locate and record the titles of easy texts, they were beginning to understand something about themselves as readers that would help them in choosing books to read independently.

Challenging Books

After the class learned to find easy books, we moved on to challenging books. For the most part, the children were able to understand when books were difficult for them to read independently. We spent many days sorting through challenging books. We decided that some were challenging even though the reader could read some of the words or repeated phrases. We also discovered that sometimes, when we thought we understood a book from the pictures, the author's text gave us much more information, and by not reading it we had missed the main idea. Once we had agreed on certain characteristics, we created a chart of challenging books. These were often titles students had not read before. They usually had several lines of text and were not easy for readers to make sense of because of their difficulty.

Just-Right Books

With strong definitions of easy books and challenging books helping us to make good choices, we next set out to define just-right books. After all our talk about easy and challenging books, it would seem that finding a just-right book would have been the easiest, but it was the most demanding. In a kindergarten classroom full of emergent readers, there was at times only a fine line between easy and just-right books. Some students were still mastering the concept of print, some were just beginning to read, and others were quickly developing independence.

As we talked together we began to sort just-right books from our other reading. We talked about what just-right books were, where to find them, and how they helped us as readers. Students soon realized that they could read easier books quickly but sometimes had to slow down with just-right books to figure something out. These were books they had read only a few times before, if at all, but they could still make sense of them and get through any challenges independently.

Conferences That Help Readers Make Good Book Choices

Books, of course, only help children learn to read if they meet children's needs. Sometimes, as I make a teaching point during a conference, I also talk about books that might be helpful in learning this new strategy or understanding. Jade, for example, was able to read books with several lines of text and more complicated story lines. Many of them contained dialogue, but her reading was mostly word-by-word. During a conference, we talked about fluency. Before I moved on I recommended some titles that might help her to practice reading as if she were talking: books with dialogue that were a bit easier and more familiar and might therefore be good places to practice reading fluently.

I also try to help students learn to balance their reading time. John, a third grader, was busy reading an Eric Carle book as I walked by his desk. This was the second day in a row I had seen him spending all his time with picture books. I stopped to talk with him. "What are you reading?" "*The Very Quiet Cricket*," he responded. "I have noticed the last few days that you have spent all your time during the workshop reading picture books." John explained that he enjoyed picture books and that Eric Carle was one of his favorite authors. Knowing that I too have a few easy books I like to read, I wrestled with myself about how best to approach this issue. I want students to read books they love, but I also want them to read books that will challenge them as readers. Picture books can challenge a third grader's thinking, but Eric Carle's probably aren't the first ones that come to mind. "Eric Carle is one of my favorite authors too," I told John, "but I'm wondering how this book helps you to be a better reader?" By asking the question I hoped to plant a seed that would help him use his time well during future workshops. After I had talked with him for a bit about balancing his reading, he finished his Eric Carle book and went back to another one he had started.

I met Brooke working in a second-grade classroom. Each day, she would place herself right at my feet during the focus lesson. She listened intently as I shared stories with her class and participated in our conversations. When students would begin to read independently, I'd look up from conferences to see her with a chapter book turning pages a little too quickly to be reading the book, and her eyes didn't seem to be moving from left to right. When she wasn't pretending to read chapter books, I'd see her roaming around the room, slowly moving from one basket to another. As I talked and read with her I quickly realized that the books she was trying to read were far too difficult for her. She wanted to read chapter books like her classmates, but chapter books weren't helping her learn to read. We all have students like Brooke in our classroom. The more time they spend reading books that are just right, the better progress they will make.

Brooke and I had several conversations during our beginning weeks together. I was honest with her. "Brooke," I said, "I understand that you want to read chapter books, but I have noticed that they are still difficult for you." Brooke nodded her head as I continued, "Reading books that are a better match will help you with your reading, and it won't be long before reading chapter books will seem easy." But words alone did not solve this problem. We also talked about books she might like to read. I brought in books I thought would appeal to her interests that looked similar to the books her friends were reading. We even found some books she would be able to read that looked more like chapter books.

My interest in her reading seemed to help. She was always eager to see what I had brought for her. In our conferences we continued to talk about the importance of balancing the reading she was doing. Her teacher, Ginny Ryland, realized the importance of helping Brooke to make better choices and adjusted the classroom library to make easier books available to her. In addition to the basket containing a variety of books that might work for Brooke and for a few other readers in the classroom, she also met with her often to teach strategies for reading increasingly challenging stories and to introduce her to new stories.

✳ Focus Lessons Developed Over Time: Balancing Reading

Teaching children to find just-right books begins in September, and and we revisit the subject throughout the year as their abilities develop and we add new genres to the classroom library. As I helped students learn to spend time with just-right books, I found that they did not immediately know how to tell which books were easy, which just right, and which challenging, but improved with time and experience. The next challenge is to teach students how to spend an appropriate amount of time with just-right books. In my classroom, students soon began rating books as easy (E), just right (JR), or challenging (CH) in their response journals, but when I reviewed their lists it soon became apparent that some were spending all their time reading easy books, others too much time attempting challenging books.

The best conversations occurred as we began to talk about how to balance our reading to include easy, just right, and difficult, but still students did not know how to be sure if their reading was balanced. I needed a way to really help students see how they were using their time and decided to use color to help make my point. I asked everyone to get out their response logs and color all the easy books on their list green, all the just-right books yellow, and all the challenging books red. I picked up a couple of these lists as we headed to the carpet for the focus lesson. Students were quick to see that all the green in Noe's book meant that he was spending most of his time with easy books. The mix of yellow and green in Matt's book helped them see that he was balancing his reading in a way that would help him to read smarter.

✳ **figure 4.5**

Spending Time with Just-Right Books.
Matt takes time to color his book log to see how he is using his time in reading.

✳ Focus Lessons: Building a Reading Life

Independent reading helps students to develop as readers, but they must understand some of the decisions that readers make in order to use their time well. During focus lessons across grade levels I have initiated conversations based on the following points.

Readers read for various purposes: Early in the year I usually bring in a stack of books I am currently reading to demonstrate all the types of reading I do. My collection usually includes a fiction book, a couple of professional texts, a magazine, a professional journal, and a poetry collection or two. As the year progresses, our conversations turn to why we read: to learn, to be entertained, to answer questions, to get important information about events, and possibly to learn how to make something.

Readers abandon books for different reasons: We have to be cautious about students who constantly abandon books, who may not know that sometimes the reward for persevering through the first chapter or two—or page or two—comes later. But sometimes books are too difficult to understand, too hard to read, or poorly written, and sometimes the content is not interesting to us.

Readers choose books of varying levels of difficulty: I'm not really sure if this is as difficult for the children as it is for us. As readers I think we understand this, but as teachers of reading I think we struggle with it. Some books I read are purely for pleasure. I enjoy a quick read as much as I enjoy a half-hour sitcom after an especially difficult day. These books are easy to read, require little brain power, and help me to relax and unwind. Some weeks these are all I can muster the ambition to read. Other times, I step up for a bit of a challenge. For example, I worked my way through *Stones from the River* by Ursula Hegi for a booktalk. It was difficult in the beginning to keep track of all the characters. I read it, stopping after nearly every chapter or two and returning to some easier reading. I am sure under normal circumstances I would have abandoned that book quickly, but after I finished it I was glad that I had stayed with it.

Readers read different genres in different ways: Novice readers need to understand that we approach different genres in different ways: We read fiction from beginning to end, but we might read only one section of a nonfiction book. Nonfiction books do not have to be read in order, and usually our purpose—to locate a fact, for example, or find out about an event—will determine the way we approach the book. When we read poetry we often skip to poems that appeal to us. I tend to read magazines from beginning to end, looking quickly through sections of little interest; I might also read only one article that has caught my attention.

Readers need to balance their reading: During the year, I help students to analyze their reading to determine whether they are spending enough time with just-right books and balancing their reading. Are students spending time only with fiction? Are students spending time only with informational texts?

Readers often read more than one book at a time: Readers read books for different reasons: a biography, a novel, a collection of nature essays, a car manual. Readers have to be careful that they don't have too many books going at one time so they are not finishing any of them.

Our interests often determine our reading: Readers like to read about topics that are interesting to them. It is easier to read books that we can connect to in some way. Our background knowledge—of the topic, the characters, or the events in a story, of an author's style or the genre—can make it easier to understand.

Readers keep a list of books they have read: Keeping a list helps us to know if we are balancing what we are reading and demonstrates where we have been as a reader. Referring to our list, we can talk about the books we have read and make recommendations to friends. Some readers also keep lists of books they plan to read in the future.

❖ Problems With Book Choice

Not too long ago I read an article by Michael Meckler entitled "Comics Are Flawed Format to Teach Reading" in our local paper. The title caught my attention immediately. Comics probably saved my brother. I doubt that he would have read at all if my grandma hadn't run to the store to purchase the latest issues of Marvel and DC comics. In the article Meckler focused on the reasons comics or, as he termed them, "graphic novels," should not be used in middle and high school classrooms to teach reading. The discussion of the value of visual literacy was interesting, but more important was his emphasis on learning to read longer texts to develop "stamina."

Although one could argue that any article about limiting reading materials in classrooms is important, this one had little relevance to primary teaching except for the last line: "With the start of the school year less than a month away, parents need to pay attention to what their children are reading in school and *whether that reading material really teaches them to read*" (my italics). The writer makes an interesting point. I struggle daily to balance helping children learn to read and helping them develop a love of reading, but they are really one and the same. Perhaps the trouble begins when we try to separate them.

The boy who loves spiders and spends every day looking through the nonfiction books about spiders that are too difficult for him but interesting will also need to read books that help him make progress as a reader. I'll search the earth for books about spiders that match his ability. I might even help him write a text about spiders that he can read. I will also appeal to his other interests and find other books at appropriate levels.

CHAPTER 5

Growing Our Libraries

Baskets of various shapes, sizes, and colors are stacked neatly on the tables in our school library. Teachers rush in after school to choose from the available selection of baskets, purchased with the help of our school P.T.O. in aid of our classroom libraries. There is an excitement in the air as teachers collaboratively reorganize libraries to support young readers.

In a meeting one afternoon we jokingly suggested that maybe our classrooms needed a "Trading Spaces" team to come in and rework the space. Our classrooms never seem large enough, and the arrangement never quite works. We are always searching for ways to use our space more effectively. Many of us have been teaching long enough to have acquired a large stash of treasures, things we will surely need one day. During this discussion our attention turned to our libraries. We are fortunate to have large book collections in our classrooms featuring authors, genres, and topics of study all thoughtfully designed to support our curriculum. But we needed to rearrange our libraries to be more appealing to our students.

One classroom from each grade level was chosen to have its library transformed by a team of teachers; when possible, grade-level teachers would work together. This seemed an efficient way to use the limited time we had, since these teachers would be familiar with the titles of books that were used, the topics of study that were part of the school year, and the needs of the children that would use this library.

At a previous meeting we had begun the conversation about our libraries, written our concerns, set goals, and devised a plan of action. Some teachers had noticed that the children in their classrooms were not using the library to support their learning. Mandy Fabb had written, "Children are having trouble selecting 'just-right' books." Lisa Callif was also concerned about the book choices her students were making. They seemed to choose the same titles over and over. Many teachers talked about the lack of nonfiction in their classrooms and the need for more

books representing other cultures. Others noted that they were constantly struggling with limited space and thought more shelves might help.

One literacy meeting wasn't enough time to completely redo our libraries, but
it provided an opportunity to make some minor adjustments. Teachers worked
quickly, and by the end of the session, noticeable improvements were apparent. The
math collection in Lisa Callif's first-grade library was now redesigned, with lami-
nated labels already in place so that students could more easily find the books they
were looking for. Ginny Ryland's second-grade library now displayed books
arranged in baskets. Sara Firestone's third-grade library highlighted some of the
authors students had studied and offered a wider range of genres for students to
visit. Molly Starkey's fourth-grade library had been reorganized to make it easier
for students to locate materials.

Our work left us wanting to spend more time. This short session had left us
with many questions. Do our libraries have books that meet the needs of all the
readers in our classrooms? How do we get students involved in this process? How
do we grow our libraries so that they continue to work for students?

※ **figure 5.1a**

Teachers Redesign Libraries. Molly Starkey and
Ginny Ryland try to find baskets to accommodate
the many sizes of the books in their classrooms.

※ **figure 5.1b**

The first-grade team took some time to redesign
Lisa Callif's math library so that students could
more easily find the books they wanted to read.

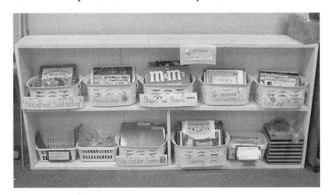

Now that my students have more time to read self-selected books, I have found that a well-organized and thoughtfully planned classroom library is essential. The library requires as much thought as any of the other instructional decisions I make. Too often books are gathered together in September and the collection remains unchanged throughout the school year. Too often, because the library has not been planned and adapted to support ongoing learning, students are unable to find the books they need or to put books back where they belong because they do not understand the system of organization. Despite the fact that nearly every professional book about teaching reading emphasizes the need for a good library, many of us *still* have libraries that cannot sustain readers. The teachers collaborated on a list of organizing principles:

- Think "outside the book" (magazines, poems, comics, ads, jokes, rhymes)
- Add picture labels to baskets
- Find places—and ways—to display books that will attract readers
- Arrange books face out so that students can easily see the covers
- Separate books by categories that fit the needs of the community
- Be sure the library is well organized and that the system is understood by everyone

Creating Libraries That Support Readers

Primary readers can be taught to make good book choices if they have ready access to a good classroom library that supports their efforts as learners. The cornerstone of our reading workshop is our library, which requires books that tap into the interests of the wide range of readers in our classroom: readers from emergent to transitional, boys to girls, native English speakers to second-language learners, bug enthusiasts to pet lovers, sports fans to poetry nuts. It has to draw readers in and invite them to sit down and stay for a while. The library influences, and is influenced by, the work taking place. When the year begins we include books that will help build community; as we study the backyard, we add informational books that help us to learn about natural life outside; as the year continues we add books that will help us learn the craft of writing. To be able to support the reading students will do, the library must grow and adapt throughout the school year.

Walking by Colleen Csiszarik's second-grade room I saw students gathered on the carpet, stacks of books spread around them, and a heated debate beginning to take shape. Colleen, never afraid to dive right in, was writing feverishly on chart paper as the class discussed a stack of books that had not yet found a basket.

Colleen's class had decided that their library was in need of some work. They wanted to add some new books, rearrange other books so they were easier to locate, and move the library around the room.

They began with books stacked at their tables, reading through titles and deciding on categories. Children working at each table came to an agreement about the books they were given and brought these categories to the group for final approval. At the end, they still had a few stacks of titles that could fit in more than one basket, and the debate raged over how to categorize them. It was decided that *Stand Tall Molly Lou Melon* by Patty Lovell was definitely a book that "teaches a lesson." Despite the fact that some students still thought it should go with "books that are funny," Devin wrapped up her case by saying, "It teaches you that it doesn't matter what people think. It only matters what you think of yourself." *Wemberly Worried* by Kevin Henkes also went into the "books that teach a lesson" stack. Brennan reminded everyone, "Kevin Henkes usually teaches a lesson."

It took some time, but finally the library was reorganized. Colleen Csiszarik found that having students involved in rearranging their library helped them to

※ **figure 5.2a**   **Thinking About the Library.** Colleen Csiszarik's second-grade students begin to categorize books for their library.

※ figure 5.2b **Second-Grade Library After Reorganization.** Colleen Csiszarik's second-grade library after the class reorganized it.

know not only what was available to read, but also how to locate the books they were interested in reading. She found more students reading from the library after their discussion, and returning books to the places where they had originated.

※ Considerations for Classroom Libraries

My classroom library has evolved over the course of my teaching because of reading I have done, teachers who have shaped my thinking, and students who understand themselves enough as readers to articulate their needs, sometimes quite adamantly. If you walk into my classroom, the library takes up at least one-fourth of the space. I have gotten rid of my desk to allow more room; I've removed a guided reading table to make more room; and I've arranged and rearranged, organized and reorganized to make more room. I think the library is that important.

While having a collection of books in our school's bookroom supports much of the small group instruction I do, it is the classroom library that supports young readers. It is in the classroom library that my students learn to love to read, to choose their reading, to connect to books, to learn from authors, and to learn from one another. It is in the classroom library that students often begin to find a reading voice. For these reasons, it is necessary to consider carefully the breadth of the collection available to students and the way they are arranged. Books should

- support student interests
- reflect the various cultures of the classroom community
- connect to students' lives and experiences
- represent topics of study
- be interesting with fascinating illustrations and magnificent language
- represent favorite authors, characters, topics

Expanding Our Libraries

Our library not only supports our workshop, it helps to build community in our classroom. As the year begins, the library is full of books that I know will inspire

figure 5.3 **Growing Our Library: Classroom Library Early in the Year.** In September, I begin with a core collection of books that will allow us to get started.

us to laugh together, wonder together, sing together, and read together. Books with beautiful language, delightful illustrations, and interesting story lines surround us and will help to provide common experiences and begin conversations. I consider books that I think students will be interested in spending time with each day; books that will draw readers in and hook them on reading.

Not only does our library help us to connect with one another, it surrounds us with authors and illustrators who will teach us throughout the year. Byron Barton's illustrations will help us learn to use shapes to draw pictures that tell a story. Lois Ehlert will teach us to explore nature, to write about things that are important to us, and to add labels to our illustrations to help our readers understand our message. Mem Fox will teach us that writers write with purpose and consider their audience.

When I first began teaching I did not have many books, but I did have library cards in a few local community libraries and added to our collection through book orders during the school year. Now I am fortunate to have a large assortment of titles. Each fall, I carefully choose a core set of books knowing that students will help me add books over the rest of the school year. I begin with books that students will be able to connect to their lives, that will support learning across content areas, and that are examples of good writing.

To draw children in, the books are arranged in baskets, covers facing out, so they can be easily flipped through. Each basket is labeled and they are never

figure 5.4

Browsing for Books. Placing books loosely in baskets, face out, allows children to browse and select books.

too full. Children are able to find and then replace books as they finish them. Early in the year I used printed basket labels, but Rachel, my organizer, suggested that we add picture labels to make it easier for everyone to find books.

At the beginning of the year, each book receives a small sticky note that matches a basket label; it sticks up above the cover so children can put books back in the basket where they belong. Before long I notice signs that the students have internalized the system; I will find books that fit into more than one category in one basket, then another. For example, a Donald Crews counting book might turn up with the math books instead of in the Crews basket, a logical placement. Tags become less necessary as students gain experience and begin to participate in the library's evolution.

Organizing the Library Early in the Year. Purple sticky notes labeled "a b c," and so on help students to know where to put books early in the year. Later these tags will no longer be necessary.

We continue to replenish books, rearranging the shelves to make room for all the voices joining our community. We add books by new authors, books on our topics of study, and titles in other categories of books suggested by readers to meet changing needs and abilities. Students show more interest in the library if new books are often added. When the reading workshop needs energy, adding a few books usually gets it moving again.

I begin the year mixing informational books and fiction together in baskets. Baskets labeled Pets, for example, will contain nonfiction books and fictional stories about cats, dogs, rabbits, and hamsters. Eventually the baskets become too full, or sorting through fiction to find the informational books we need for study too time-consuming. When this happens we pull out the informational books and sort them into categories. When we begin to sort the informational books, I make a big deal about it. We get out more baskets and find a separate place to shelve nonfiction so that it can be found easily. We talk about topics we'd like to see included and make new labels.

⁕ **figure 5.6** **Nonfiction Library.** Having a separate section for nonfiction helps students to begin to consider the characteristics of informational books.

Some of the best ways I know for expanding and enriching classroom libraries include these points:

- provide opportunities for students to have a say in the library
- change the books often
- adjust the library collection to meet readers' ever-changing needs
- have books by favorite authors or featuring favorite characters available
- keep familiar books where students can easily revisit them
- include a wide variety of genres
- think about including comics, poetry cards, jokes, ads, and magazines
- include books that are part of a series

⁕ Leveled Books

I struggle constantly with the issue of leveled books in our classroom library. Having books that students can read independently is essential, but students are not always interested in spending time with leveled text. I have seen classrooms in which tubs labeled with guided reading levels from A–O line the floor, each container home for a separate letter. I have seen classroom libraries that consist almost entirely of leveled books and classroom libraries that don't have a sufficient number of books at varying levels to meet the demands of the students.

Because primary students are learning to read, they need just-right books, but let's put leveled books into perspective for a minute. Leveled books are a tool intended to help teachers in choosing books for guided reading lessons by grouping those with similar supports and challenges together. It is crucial, however, to remember the limitations of this system: It doesn't know our readers. It cannot consider the background knowledge readers bring to the book, the strategies being used, or the language experience of the individual child.

Early one morning, from the other side of the bookroom, I heard a long sigh. A teacher searching for books for a group of readers was clearly frustrated. "This leveling system doesn't always make sense. These students are reading at a level N according to the benchmark assessment, but when I brought a level N book to them they couldn't read it." It took me many months to realize the significance of what she had said. As I conferred with older readers I realized how important prior knowledge is in reading and understanding vocabulary. A book introduction can sometimes help students to read successfully, but not all "level N" books will work for all "level N" readers.

The limitations of leveling are especially apparent in nonfiction. Teachers trying to match readers to levels will have a difficult time giving a student the same level fiction and nonfiction books. The content, vocabulary, and structure of a nonfiction text are often more challenging and require more support. In choosing books for readers, try to recall what the student may already know.

From my experience with Reading Recovery I know that leveled texts can support instruction and make it easier

※ **figure 5.7**

A Mixed Collection with Some Leveled Text. It is often easier for students to locate just-right books in a collection that varies in difficulty.

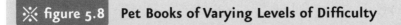

✳ figure 5.8   Pet Books of Varying Levels of Difficulty

Our Dog Sam by Ron Bacon
Where's Spot by Eric Hill
Franklin Wants a Pet by Paulette Bourgeois
Sammy at the Farm by Kathleen Urmston and Karen Evans
Where Is the Cat? by Dianne Frasier and Constance Compton
The Old Dog by Charlotte Zolotow
The Stray Dog by Marc Simont
Bad Dog Max! by Marina Windsor
Taking Care of Rosie by Lynn Salem and Josie Stewart
Follow Carl! By Alexandra Day
Dressed Up Sammy by Kathleen Urmston and Karen Evans

to choose books. I also know that level is not the only factor determining read-ability. I have to know my readers. I need to consider the prior knowledge the child brings to the story, the layout of the pages, the vocabulary, the amount of support the illustrations provide, and the structure of the story. I know the importance of a good match between the reader and the book, and that it isn't always about the level.

Students, especially novice readers, do need to be able to locate books they can read successfully. The best arrangement for leveled books has been to set up several baskets with a selection of books with similar characteristics so that children still have the flexibility to choose. For example, we have collected a basket of books in our classroom library for emergent readers. These readers need books with few words, a text set in a consistent place on the page, and strong picture support.

Unfortunately, baskets of leveled books do not always attract readers. I have had more success getting students to read these books if they are interfiled with nonleveled books. For example, a collection of pet books contained titles of various levels of difficulty. Children who wanted to read a just-right book could find one in the pet basket. I think it is actually easier for some readers to choose a just-right book from among a collection of books that vary widely in range of difficulty than from a basket of very similar books.

Leveled Books and Libraries

Labeled baskets filled with books that reflect the varied levels of learners in the classroom, the range of interests, the breadth of the curriculum, and the diversity of the students line the shelves of Michelle Watts' first-grade classroom library. Books by favorite authors, books with wonderful language, and books that reach into the hearts of students rest face out along the front wall of the room. Across the room in a cozy corner are books that any junior scientist or world traveler would love to spend time with, while another corner is filled with baskets of books organized according to the concepts important to budding mathematicians. The bright colors and large open spaces invite readers to sit down for a while and read.

Michelle was concerned that her first-grade students were spending almost all of their reading time with picture books that were often too difficult for them to read independently, instead of balancing their reading time with other kinds of reading. I wasn't surprised. If given the choice, kindergarten and first-grade students would rather spend time with picture books than leveled text. Who can blame them? The illustrations in picture books are often colorful and detailed, and the books have interesting story lines that students can usually figure out by looking at the pictures. Leveled texts, on the other hand, often have simple pictures and basic story structures. Michelle knew that picture books were interesting to students and contributed to a love of reading, but she also wanted them to read books at their own independent level, books that would help them build on the strategies and understandings they would need to read increasingly challenging texts.

Michelle decided to talk with her students about the importance of spending more of their workshop time reading books that were "just right" for them. But first she needed a better way to organize her leveled books so that students would want to read them and could access them easily. We didn't want kids wandering around the room looking for a "level F" book, and we certainly didn't want students saying to each other, "I'm reading a level H book and you are still reading level D books." How could we help them to know which books would benefit them as readers? How could we talk to them about balancing their reading?

Leveled texts had originally been stored in baskets, each containing a different level, with a picture label on the front. We noticed certain common characteristics of books across levels and began to develop a plan to set up baskets of books for different types of readers. Once we had considered the previous focus of her instruction, we looked at her class list and placed her students in three groups, each group having similar needs. In three baskets we then placed the books, each containing several levels of text. Using a different color for each basket, we placed a sticky note inside the front cover at the top of each book so that students could easily match it to the correct basket. Because these books weren't sorted by author, topic, or genre, marking them like this helped to ensure that they went back to their basket.

Michelle hoped that her students would figure out which basket was "just right" for them. The first basket contained books that, for the most part, would be a good fit for novice readers. These readers were just developing beginning reading strategies and had a core set of known words. They needed simple text with pictures that supported their reading. The second basket contained books with several lines of text. Readers who used this basket would be reading for meaning, monitoring, and beginning to self-correct. The language in these books was somewhat predictable but the text still required effort to read and understand it. The pictures supported the reading, but readers would have to balance their use of meaning and visual cues to read successfully. The final basket was intended for the most experienced readers, who were reading for meaning and flexible in how they approached unfamiliar texts. The books in this basket were not as predictable and required higher-level strategies for comprehension.

Respecting Readers

Allison taught me a lot about book choice in the classroom. She came to kindergarten with a lot of experience with books. When I'd pull out a book for a read-aloud, she often said, "I love this one. We have it at home." During one of the first weeks of school, as we talked about reading during our focus lesson, I threw out a question: "Why do we read?" A silence hung in the air—one of those moments when you know the lesson has already gone too far and it is time to backpedal. Then Allison spoke up. "Sometimes we read to learn." She smiled. I could have danced! It's always nice to have someone save a lesson gone astray.

Although Allison came to kindergarten already very experienced with books, she wasn't yet reading. I'll never forget the first time I tried to get her to spend some time reading leveled text during independent reading. Holding a few books I thought would be appropriate, I stopped to confer with her. I tried the "I brought you some books I thought you might like" approach. "Do you see a couple you might like to add to your box to read?" Allison looked up at me, a picture book in her hand. "I don't like those kind of books." She returned to her picture book and went on with her reading. "What don't you like about them?" I asked. "I have to read those at home," she replied.

I could tell Allison was not going to be an easy sell, but I also knew that she would learn to read with or without me. I hunted through the library for picture books I thought she might be able to read and managed to find a few leveled text about dogs and cats I thought I might be able to tempt her with. A few days later I tried again, "Allison, I have been thinking a lot about the things you like to read. I know from your stories that you like to write about your pets, so I brought you a few of my favorite pet books." I proceeded to give her a quick summary of each of the books I had in my hand. She smiled and chose a couple, not all of them of course. She wanted to make sure that I understood who was in charge of her reading. I learned to respect Allison's reading choices, and she learned to balance her reading.

CHAPTER 6

Weaving Reading and Writing Workshops Together

I will never forget my move from first-grade to kindergarten teaching. At the time I wasn't just changing grade levels, I was leaving the school district in which I had spent most of my learning and teaching life. There were only two elementary schools in the small community where I had not only gone to school but taught the children of old friends and neighbors in grades one to six. Soon I would be teaching in a city that had thirteen elementary schools. It had taken much soul searching, but I had finally decided to leave my position teaching first grade and Reading Recovery to work as a literacy coordinator and teacher in a large district not far from my home.

The move from first grade to kindergarten was not the biggest grade-level jump I had made. However, I recognized that there would be significant differences in teaching kindergarten students, many concerned with issues of independence and experience. In my first-grade teaching I had been using the literacy framework from *Guided Reading,* by Irene Fountas and Gay Su Pinnell, to support learning in my classroom. This included read-alouds, shared reading, and guided reading to support reading instruction. It seemed this framework would work in a kindergarten classroom as well.

I knew my reading instruction would easily fit into a kindergarten program, but I wondered if these young students could work in a writer's workshop. Since my first year of teaching I had used the writer's workshop with student writers. No matter the grade level, from first to sixth, the workshop had allowed me to support all my students in their learning. The flexibility of this apprenticeship model made it possible for me to find the time to meet the needs of individual students while permitting them to take ownership of their work.

Despite nearly fifteen years of teaching experience, I was nervous about the start of the school year. How would I arrange the day for these young learners? In August our district offered a week of training for new staff. It was comforting to know that I would spend one of these days with an experienced kindergarten teacher, who would discuss curriculum and learning for these new-to-school children. Hoping to lower my August anxiety, I was looking forward to beginning to develop a plan. Prepared with a long list of questions as the day began, I listened closely as Gayle Brand, a district literacy specialist who had been teaching kindergarten students for several years, began to arm us with survival tips that would, at the very least, keep us alive for the first six weeks of school.

As Gayle talked with us I began to feel some relief, but my list of questions still weighed heavy in my hands. She must have sensed the uneasiness of her audience, because she decided to address our concerns. Glancing at my long list, I looked at her. "Do you use a writer's workshop in your kindergarten classroom?" Having used the workshop from grades one to six, my hope was that before the year was over my kindergarten students would be able to use the workshop as well. With hardly a pause she looked me square in the eye and said, "From the first day." I nearly fell over. These kids were going to come into my classroom, some without any school experience, not writing, perhaps not knowing letters, and possibly not even knowing how to write their name. How was I going to get through the first day? How would I teach them to work within a workshop? I decided that if Gayle said it could be done, it could be done, and dived in head first, no water in the pool, on the first day. I must admit that I was a little apprehensive. How would students manage the workshop with so little experience?

To my surprise the workshop was integrated into our classroom routine with relative ease from the very beginning. On the first day of school, since we were all getting to know one another, the children began by writing about something they thought others would want to know about them. Most used pictures to tell their story, although I noticed as I walked around talking with students, that a few had attempted to add print. As we shared our writing at the end of the day, I knew they were hooked. In the days that followed students learned to listen to one another as they began their journey toward understanding the world of print and their place within it, developing a sense of story that would help them connect reading and writing to their lives and to each other.

During that first year of teaching kindergarten, I was amazed at what children showed me they could do. By the time December rolled around their writing exceeded my expectations. I had to work to stay ahead of the class. Students were writing to tell the stories of their lives. Their illustrations were beginning to show an understanding of the importance of detail as well as knowledge about characters and setting. They were attempting to add words to support their pictures with a success appropriate for what they knew about print.

※ figure 6.1a   **September Writing.** Taelor tells us about her sandbox.

※ figure 6.1b   **September Writing.** Robert tells us about riding a scooter at daycare.

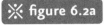 **December Writing.** Taelor tells us about playing with her new friend, Katie.

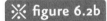 **December Writing.** Robert tells us that his family got a new car.

Students had time to write independently each day, but at the time, they did not have a similar opportunity to read independently for extended periods. I noticed that while demonstrating all of this knowledge in writing, they were not using what they had learned about print in their reading. Some words they could write down, they could not consistently read. They could record the sounds of words but did not draw on this information in their reading. Most important, they were writing to make meaning, but they did not seem to understand that we also read to make meaning. Where had I gone wrong?

As winter turned to spring that first year, the trend continued. I realized that many of these novice readers were not setting themselves up to read new books. If I didn't introduce a book, they didn't attempt to understand it on their own. They were writing independently and with confidence using what they knew, but they were not as confident in their reading. Why weren't they connecting what they knew in writing to their reading?

As I thought about it, I realized that our writer's workshop had an energy lacking from our reading time. I knew how much they understood about words, language, and language craft. They had written about their families, their interests, and what made them laugh and cry. I knew their stories. Each conversation we had together seemed to interweave with the one before and the one that followed. We had developed a community centered in this writing, but we had not extended that community into our reading. They had found reasons to write, but I hadn't really helped them to find reasons to read.

Students understood the power of their pencils to tell their stories. We heard about Rachel's first bike ride without training wheels, David's new baby sister, and the day that Sandra's cat died. We all knew that Cameron loved, loved, loved dinosaurs. Not only could he name them all and tell loads of facts about each kind, he could nearly write *tyrannosaurus*, despite the fact that he was still learning to write words like *look*. Peter taught us how to take care of a hamster, Chris helped us to know what would be required if we were considering the purchase of a lizard, and Yakira made sure we understood the needs of our pet dogs.

The enthusiasm I witnessed as students wrote and shared their stories, I began to realize, was not as evident in their reading. I had to find ways to connect the stories in their hearts to the stories in the books that surrounded us. Through guided reading they were becoming better readers by assessment standards, yet they hadn't all developed a love of reading or an understanding of reasons to read. At the time, I hadn't looked beyond guided reading, but my observations led me to change gears. I adjusted our schedule to allow more time for independent reading from self-selected text. Then, knowing that reading and writing are reciprocal processes, I looked for ways to use students' writing to enhance reading instruction. I asked myself several defining questions:

- How can I connect the conversations in both the reading and writing workshops?
- What can I learn about the readers in my classroom through their writing?
- What can students learn about reading through writing?
- How can we use writing to think about and respond to reading?

Connecting Conversations Across Workshops

Because reading and writing are related processes, much of our teaching can be applied in both contexts, from one workshop to the other. Print concepts, strategies for telling and understanding stories, knowledge of story structures and genres, vocabulary, and the uses of literacy can inform both reading and writing. When possible, I always try to link the learning students are doing in both, so they clearly see the connections between creating a message and making sense of one. At times, the line between the two workshops blurs. It is not uncommon for me to walk into the reading workshop to find students writing down their reaction to reading in their reading notebooks, recording something important they want to remember, or jotting down a new idea. Likewise, it is not uncommon for me to find students in the writing workshop browsing through the book baskets for support from favorite authors or reading to find out more about the topic they have chosen to write about.

When possible, to strengthen student understanding of these processes, I connect the teaching of both workshops. From listening to my kindergarten students' predictions ("What might happen next?") I realized that they needed to understand that many stories involve a problem, a place where the story begins to change. Often they are better able to make connections to reading by using what they know about real life, so we began by talking about problems we had solved in our classroom, as well as the problems we encountered in familiar stories we had read together often: in *The Recess Queen* by Alexis O'Neill, *Thomas' Snowsuit* by Robert Munsch, and *Wishy-Washy Day* by Joy Cowley, for example. During read-alouds and shared reading we began to look for the places in stories where the problem begins and the story starts to change. At the same time we began looking at the stories children were writing during writer's workshop. The problem in

Kanna's story was that her tooth needed to come out but she was scared because it was her first loose tooth. The problem in Yakira's story was that she found an egg from a nest on the ground. The problem in David's story was that his baby sister was always crying. Conversations in both workshops helped students to begin to make better predictions about the story line.

One day, working with Michelle Watts in her first-grade classroom during a writing lesson, I noticed the close relationship between the teaching in her reading and in her writing focus lessons. Michelle had asked me to come to her classroom during writing workshop to take a look at her students' writing: their stories were just touching the surface, the sentences were short, and the details limited. For her focus lesson she had written a three-page story with a short sentence about her dog on each. Students listened as she read her story. Michelle then added more detailed sentences to each page, showing students how the additional words made her story more interesting. As we walked around the classroom afterward, as students wrote, we looked for writers who might be ready to take this next step.

I stayed in the classroom for their reading workshop, listening as Michelle talked about mental images. She wanted her students to understand that the words authors use help us to visualize the story. Michelle would read, stopping to talk about words and phrases that created visual images, which she called "mind pictures."

As we sat down that afternoon to look at pieces of student writing, we talked about the reading and writing workshop lessons for that day. The two lessons had been so similar. We needed to help students to see this link. Students needed to know that writers don't just add random details to a story, they choose words that give the reader a vivid "mind picture." Authors use words to create a picture in the reader's mind, to tell us more; as writers they needed to do this too. We began looking at words and phrases in published books and student writing that evoked pictures in our minds. During Michelle's writer's workshop the next day, she made this connection clear to students, challenging them to use words and details that would give readers a good mind picture.

I notice many opportunities to connect the teaching in the focus lessons in both workshops. We begin the year with conversations in both workshops that help us learn to live and work together. In later discussions, we read like writers, looking at the decisions authors make to strengthen their message and thinking more critically about reading. Lessons intersect across workshops as we develop strategies for helping ourselves with reading and writing. Finally, our conversations weave together, shaping our lives as readers and writers.

✳ figure 6.3   Connecting Focus Lessons: Teaching for Understanding

Comprehension Strategies	In Writing: Considerations for Writing Student as Author	In Reading: Looking at Mentor Text
Reading and Writing for Understanding	• What do you want your reader to understand or know? • Are there places where the writing is confusing?	• What is the message the author wants us to understand or know? • Are there places where the reading is confusing?
Connecting	• How do your connections with books help you to write? • What do you write about?	• What topics do authors write about? • How do authors choose their topics?
Questioning	• What will readers want to know?	• What do you expect the author to tell you?
Visualizing	• Which words will help your readers to picture your story?	• What words do authors use to help readers to picture the story?
Inferring	• Where can you say it without really saying it?	• How do authors say it without really saying it?
Determining Importance	• What details do you need to add to your writing? • What are the important events in your story? • Who are the important characters? • What is important for your reader to know?	• What important details do authors include in their stories? • What are the important events in the story? • Who are the important characters? • What do you think the author wants you to know?

▶

❊ figure 6.3 continued

Comprehension Strategies	In Writing: Considerations for Writing Student as Author	In Reading: Looking at Mentor Text
Synthesizing	• Where does your story change? • What revisions would help improve your message?	• What did the author tell you that caused you to change your mind?
Genre	• What features, structures, or elements should you include in your writing in this genre to improve your message?	• What features, structures, or elements are unique to this genre? • How do they strengthen the message?

❊ figure 6.4   Connecting Focus Lessons: Strategies for Independence

	In Writing: Ways Smart Writers Help Themselves	In Reading: Ways Smart Readers Help Themselves
Using Picture Cues	How do illustrations help us to strengthen our message? • Writers use pictures to tell more about their story. • Writers need pictures that match their words. • Writers add details to their illustration that will tell their readers more.	How do illustrations help us to understand the story? • Illustrators create pictures that tell more about the story. • Illustrators create pictures that go with the story. • Illustrators add details that often tell us more about the story. ▶

✳ **figure 6.4 continued**		
	In Writing: **Ways Smart Writers** **Help Themselves**	**In Reading:** **Ways Smart Readers** **Help Themselves**
Balancing Cues	• Writers make sure their writing makes sense and looks right.	• Readers make sure their reading makes sense and looks right.
Rereading	• Writers go back and read to make sure their writing looks right and makes sense. • Writers go back and read to make sure their message is clear. • Writers go back and read to revise and edit their writing.	• Readers go back and read when they are stuck. • Readers go back and read when they don't understand. • Readers go back and read to fix their reading.
Monitoring and Self-Correcting	• Writers notice when their writing doesn't make sense or look right and try to fix it.	• Readers notice when their reading doesn't make sense and try to fix it.

✳ Mentor Texts

In *Radical Reflections*, Mem Fox tells us, "The gains we make as writers, from hearing literature read aloud, aren't bound by form. Rhythm and vocabulary transcend form: they're tools of power that can be transported easily from one genre to the next according to our needs" (p. 113). The conversations we have about books, the genres that we share, and the authors that we study help support the student writers in the classroom by giving them ideas for topics, ways to use words, and structures that will help in their writing.

Students moved back to their seats after our writing focus lesson. We had just finished talking about making sure our writing and illustrations are a good match, and I was ready to begin conferring with students.

Some grabbed a new piece of paper; others began to reread yesterday's work as they settled into their writing. Austin hung back a bit and walked beside me. With a broad smile he said, "Mrs. Mere, I know what I'm going to write about today." I wasn't surprised. Austin was one of the first students to understand that our best writing ideas come to us outside the writing workshop. He quickly learned to look at the things happening around him and save the ideas for his writing. "I'm going to write about groundhogs," he said triumphantly. I stopped, looked at him, and quickly thought about the significance of what he had said. This was the first time I had heard him talk about writing a nonfiction piece, although as I thought more about what he said I was only surprised that he hadn't said it before. Austin loved nonfiction. When we developed our nonfiction section earlier in the year, he was excited as we discussed ideas that would help us sort the books so they were easy to find. The shark books caught his eye first, and he was hooked. Soon Austin could be found during the reading workshop sitting at a small table near the nonfiction section with a few friends, discussing all that they were learning as they read.

Austin's idea not only moved him forward as a writer; I knew it could help our entire class. Many students in the classroom who enjoyed reading books about insects and animals might also like to try to write about what they were learning so that others could read their work. I shared Austin's story the next day during our focus lesson and watched eyes begin to twinkle as students thought about the possibilities for their writing that Austin had just given to them—and, of course, the idea is always better when it comes from a peer.

Books we read during the reader's workshop become a part of our conversations in the writer's workshop. Although it was nonfiction that changed Austin's writing, it was a book's structure that helped Kinsey tell readers how to care for cats. Kinsey loved books about cats and spent weeks reading about how to care for her pet at home. Using the format of the pages of a book she had read, she wrote her own story about caring for a cat. The books we had shared during focus lessons in the reader's workshop as well as the books she had read during independent reading had given Kinsey a way to share her message with others.

✷ figure 6.5

Using Mentor Text.
Kinsey used a format
similar to those we
had seen in nonfiction
books to tell us how
to care for a cat.

✷ Connecting Reading and Writing for Students

During reading conferences I learn about readers, but I also pay attention to what
I can learn about readers in writing conferences. Kneeling down beside Nazarena
for a writing conference, I take a look at her story. Her book contains three pages.
Each contains a few people floating in a sea of letters. The letters are a mix of cap-
ital and lowercase letters written in long strings without spacing. Nazarena has
taken note of our discussions about how words can help us tell our stories and has
tried to add sentences to her writing like many of her friends at the table. But hers
are really random letter strings. "You've been working hard," I say, as I look through
her story, knowing that this is the first time she has attempted to add any writing
to her story independently. Nazarena smiles and acknowledges that this has been a
lot of work. "Can you tell me about your story?" I ask.

Nazarena turns to the first page and says, "My mom got a new car." She turns to the next page and says, "I went to my grandma's." Finally, she turns to the last page and says, "My sister is crying." When I talk with Nazarena for a bit about the content of her story, it becomes obvious that these are three unconnected stories, yet Nazarena has put them together in the same book. I have already noticed in reading conferences that Nazarena often talks about each page of a book as if it is unrelated to the page before. "Are you finished with this story?" I inquire. Nazarena proudly nods in affirmation. I am going to need to help Nazarena develop her sense of story, but I decide that this is not the time to do it. Knowing that she is ready to move on to a new story, I decide to celebrate this work, but I put her on my list for a first conference tomorrow.

The next day during writer's workshop Nazarena begins a new story. "I'll need three pages," she tells me. Grabbing three pages, I ask her to tell me about her story. "My dad is holding my kitty." I move the second page in front of her. "Tamarah is my friend," she responds. "My mom is having a birthday."

"You have a lot to write about." I smile as I grab *Goldilocks and the Three Bears*, a familiar story that I have heard Nazarena retell during reader's workshop. "Stories are usually about one thing." Reaching into her browsing bag of familiar books, I continue, "This story, *The Way We Go to School*, is about the way children go to school each day. This story, *Huggles' Breakfast*, is about all the things that Huggles eats for breakfast." Picking up *Goldilocks and the Three Bears* I tell Nazarena, "This story is about what happens when Goldilocks visits the bears' house."

"You have three great ideas for a story, but they are three different ideas. Which one do you think you most want to write about?" I ask, repeating her earlier ideas. "My mom's birthday," Nazarena replies quickly. "Tell me about her birthday."

"I helped my mom decorate her cake."

"That will be a great way to start your story," I tell her, placing a piece of paper on her mat. "Then what did you do?"

Nazarena thinks for a moment. "I helped my dad decorate the house."

"I'll bet it looked great. What did you decorate it with? Balloons? Signs?" I mentally kick myself as soon as the words come out of my mouth. It is obvious that Nazarena is really working hard to think about her responses, and the last thing I want to do is get her off track.

"We used lots of colors," she replies.

I'm a bit uncertain about what she means, but I want her to stay focused on the topic so I continue, "You helped your dad decorate the house. That will be the second page."

"Then the people came," Nazarena adds, as I place another piece of paper on the pile.

I pause for a minute to see if she is finished. "Then we had a party." She grins.

"That will be a great ending," I say, smiling. "Let's see if I understand. This book is all about your mom's birthday. First, you helped your mom make a cake. Then you helped your dad decorate the house. Finally, the people came and you had a party."

"Yes," she says, grabbing her pencil as I staple her three pages together. I talk her through the story one more time to be sure she is ready to write, and I jot down her story in my notebook, knowing that it will take her a few days to complete it. For the next few days I will check in with her quickly at the start of the workshop to see how the writing is going.

This is just the beginning of helping Nazarena to develop a sense of story. I know we will need to have other conversations during reading workshop to help her recognize that stories often have a beginning, a middle, and an end. Retelling familiar stories will be a good way to start; later, showing her how to look through the pictures before she reads new stories will help her begin to connect events as she prepares to read.

Approaching writing conferences with a reading teacher's eye allows me to see what students understand about both reading and writing. Writing provides a window into reading: I see what a child understands, what a child nearly understands, and what is next in that child's learning. Looking at writing can tell me what students know about print, about words, and about putting a message down on paper. It can tell me whether they have the ability to develop a story, to sequence events, or to notice detail. I can discover what students understand about story language and their accumulated vocabulary.

Conferring with a Reading Teacher's Eye

Having writing conferences with a reading teacher's eye also allows me to help learners make connections between reading and writing. During conversations with students in the writer's workshop I can compare what a student knows in writing and reading and consider the strengths in one that may support the other. Instead of teaching the reader during reading conferences and the writer during writing conferences, I look for opportunities in both workshops to teach the learner.

Sometimes I notice that students know something in writing that would help them to make progress in reading. I sat down beside Matt during a writing conference to help him with his story. He was writing about falling off his bike while trying to make a difficult turn. As he wrote "This is what I fell like," he was able to record the beginning letter of each word accurately with the exception of *fell*; here he recorded a *v* for an *f*, a not uncommon mix-up since we make the sounds the same way when we speak. Even though he was using this information in his writing, as I conferred with him during the reading workshop I noticed that he did not use the beginning letters to attempt to read unknown words.

Over the course of our next reading conferences I began to show Matt how to use the beginning letter of words to monitor his reading and figure out the ones he didn't know. When Matt made a meaningful attempt, even though the beginning letter did not match, I would wait. At first he didn't notice, so I used a very supportive prompt: "What you said made sense, but it didn't look right." He responded more quickly to a direct prompt: "That didn't look right. Try it again." When he stopped at an unknown word I reminded him, "Try something that makes sense and starts like that letter." Matt's writing conference helped me to see what he was ready to learn in his reading conference. When he wrote, he understood that the beginning letters in words had to match the sound he heard, but he needed to pay more attention to this visual information in his reading.

❖ Teaching About Words in Writing

In *Becoming Literate* (1991), Marie Clay explains, "Features of the written code become more obvious to the child when he attempts to put his ideas into writing for someone else to receive, than when he tries to receive (read) someone else's ideas" (p. 97). Of course primary children need to learn about how words work. As primary-grade teachers, we knew this long before the National Reading Panel completed its study. However, children also need to learn how to weigh this visual information against the meaning of the text.

I once watched as a child received any number of visual prompts as he was reading a new story, each one specific to solving that word only. The prompts went something like this: "When two vowels go walking, the first one…," "That's an *e* at the end," "It could be *brit*, but it is *bright*," and so on. Here the child's first attempt in all these examples used visual information, and the teacher further prompted with visual information. Two things were obvious: First, this child could more effectively be using meaning to help figure out what would make sense, and second, the child is obviously confused about the ways vowels work in words. Her confusion might be resolved through word study and work in writing. Spending so much time on word work in a story can interfere with understanding, which can complicate reading for some students.

In addition to providing teachers concrete examples of what students know about words, writing offers children an opportunity to learn about words. According to Marie Clay, "While a child is creating a story in print, the eye and the brain are directed to important features [of print]" (p. 109). In primary classrooms it makes sense to see students' writing as an opportunity to teach them about the way words work.

Writing as a Tool for Thinking About Reading

Janet Angelillo (2003) defines a reader's notebook as follows: "A reading journal serves the purpose of proving to the teacher that the student has read the book by requiring students to write summaries or retellings after most or every reading session, to record the time spent and number of pages read, and to predict or ask questions. However, the reader's notebook differs in that it is for the reader's benefit" (p. 47). When Abby asks if she can draw a picture of the setting the author of her chapter book describes, the notebook is her own. When Robert creates a map of the places mentioned in the book he is reading, the notebook is his own. When students like Donta ask if they can write down a great line from their reading, they are making the notebook their own. Each year some students enjoy writing unprompted responses in their notebooks. Sharing these thoughts with the classroom community usually inspires a small group of students to give it a try, but for some students it is too much work. I honor students' feelings on this. The last thing I want to do is make someone not want to read.

I don't keep a reader's notebook myself. Instead I jot down my reactions to my reading in my writer's notebook. Sometimes I share these with my students. I don't write about everything I read, as I find that tedious, but I do take time to record what catches my attention. Sometimes it is a line, and I jot it quickly in my book. For example, I loved these words from *The Secret Life of Bees* by Sue Monk Kidd: "Stories have to be told or they die, and when they die, we can't remember who we are or why we're here." This was a favorite from *Seabiscuit* by Laura Hillenbrand: "He was eastern born and bred, but he had a westerner's restlessness." Sometimes something I have read sparks an idea for my own writing, and I play with this idea in my notebook.

Writing not only teaches students about words that may be useful in their reading, it also helps readers to remember and extend their thinking as they read. In *Explorations in Language Acquisition and Use* (2003), Stephen Krashen notes, "When we write, we attempt to represent our cognitive structures, our current thoughts, on the page. The act of doing this is a powerful stimulus toward creating new cognitive structures, new ideas" (p. 73). In our school building teachers have struggled over response notebooks in hallway chats, literacy meetings, and booktalks. Do students need to keep a response notebook? Should they write in their notebook every day? What should be kept in the notebook? These have been difficult questions, and we have all found the answers that work in our own classrooms. Many responses are drawings, so even my kindergarten students can keep a notebook. Entries don't have to be long retellings or summaries. I don't want my students to spend all their reading time writing down their reactions, but I have found that they enjoy recording their thinking and sharing it with their peers.

In some classrooms it is common practice for students to write a daily letter to their teacher about their reading. When I first began providing more time for independent reading, I asked students to keep a response notebook for accountability purposes—if students were going to be given so much time to read books of their choice I needed to know that they were using their time wisely. Students chose from a list of possible responses or summarized their reading, and I went through the notebooks. What I found was that students were spending too much of their reading time writing responses. Honestly, it didn't take student responses to determine who was having difficulty reading: a quick look around the room provided all the information I needed.

Then I began to use student response notebooks to collect evidence of understanding. For example, if I was teaching students about questioning, I would have them make a two-column chart. On one side they would write their questions, on the other, their answers. That way I could check to see how well they understood this new strategy and how well they were able to use it to enhance their reading. Now most of the required writing we do is in response to read-alouds and shared reading. I find that having students respond to common experiences helps me to compare one student's understanding with that of others, provides opportunities for conversation, and gives everyone something to say. I still have students demonstrate their understanding of the new strategies and concepts we are learning or respond to their reading in a way that shows they comprehend the author's message, but through conversations they are learning to make their notebooks a tool for their own thinking.

✻ figure 6.6a

Response to Reading. Randi got her idea for writing after reading *Boo to a Goose* by Mem Fox.

✻ figure 6.6b

Response to Reading. Sara used the structure of *Guess What?* by Mem Fox to tell us that she can skate.

※ figure 6.7

Alekya's Learning About Daffodils. Alekya uses her notebook to record new learning.

DAFFODIL				
You	will	see		DaffoDils
come	first	in	the	
spring.	DAFFoDiiS	grow	from	
BUlBs.	BUlBs	live	For	A
long	time.	BUlBs	of	
made	in	fall.	thay	
stay	quiet	in	the	
winter.	if	it	is	warm
thay	grow	thay	pop	
out	in	the	sunshine.	

DanDe Lion			
People	Dont	like to	see
Brite	flowers.	the	dandelion
is	a	weeD.	its long thick
roots	macK	it	harD to
Pull	out	the	weeD.
after	it	has	BlooMed
the	thay	are	recPlaced
White.	now	the	Plant
looks	Deferant.	people	can
Blow	A	DanDeLion.	people
Eat	DanDeLions	in	soup.
thay	Put	it	in SaleDs
to.			

Early one spring afternoon we took a walk around our school building in search of signs of spring. We were continuing our conversation about the natural life in our backyard and the changes that take place with the seasons. As we returned to the classroom Alekya asked, "What is the difference between a dandelion and a daffodil?" Resisting the urge to simply answer her question, I suggested that she try to find out and sent her off to look in a few books that might help her. Alekya could read nearly everything in sight but spent most of her time with fiction. Her search for informational text would not only extend the teaching I had been doing with her about questioning, it would also send her to nonfiction, a genre she had spent little time with up to now. As Alekya began to seek out information I suggested that she might want to record what she was learning so she could tell us about it later. She liked the idea. As she began to record her learning about dandelions and daffodils, other students began to try to do the same.

My hope is that as the year progresses students will find ways to make writing about reading work for them.

CHAPTER 7

Using Assessment to Guide Our Teaching

I used to do most of my daily reading assessment during guided-reading groups, as I listened and worked with students. When I noticed something that called for more information, I would pull students aside and take a running record as they read a benchmark book. Most of my reading instruction was based on the information I had gathered in these two contexts. That's not to say that I didn't notice the work students did during other parts of the day, just that I wasn't as intentional about watching and listening as I am now. Yet my observations in these two contexts did not tell me enough about students' learning. I knew about how they were making sense of unfamiliar books, but I didn't know how they were thinking about their reading or what their interests were as readers.

Perhaps coaching has helped me with observation. I walk into classrooms at many different times, and it has become second nature for me to start to look for signs of what students know about literacy as soon as I enter. I often learn as much about a student's reading by watching as by listening. Looking around the classroom I watch individual children for signs of engagement and independence. What is the child reading? Is the child caught up in the book? Is the child working alone or with others? At what pace does the child seem to be reading?

Slowing down enough to listen, observe, record, and reflect on the information I have gathered has become part of my day. Throughout focus lessons, during the conversations in conferences, in small-group lessons, and in share sessions, I listen and record what I see along with snippets of talk. Taking notes as children read, looking carefully at their daily writing, listening to their responses and questions during shared reading and read-aloud and as they work throughout the day all provide insights to inform my decision making and planning.

My basic goal is to determine if students are able to read for understanding. If students are having a difficult time reading for understanding, especially primary readers, I attempt to determine whether it is an issue of decoding or an issue of comprehension. If students are able to understand their reading, then I think about how I can extend the learning for these children. In addition to monitoring student understanding, I also consider how students are using their time in the workshop, the strategies they are using, and the decisions they are making as readers. The assessment chart in Figure 7.1 shows some of the questions I ask myself as I observe and talk with readers.

Assessing Understanding Through Conversations

It is nearly lunch time on the first day back from winter break, and students are beginning to file out of their classrooms laughing and talking with one another. Excitement is in the air. Walking beside Molly Starkey, a colleague across the hall, I ask, "How's the first day back?" She smiles. "This is my favorite day of the year. The students are excited to be here, and they already know our routines!" I nod in agreement and walk into my classroom to get ready for the arrival of my students, excited about hearing the stories of what has happened in their lives over the last few weeks and looking forward to beginning again.

I love January! It feels much like the first days of the school year, full of the excitement of returning as well as the anticipation of all that is to come. While everyone is making resolutions to improve their lives, for me, it is the perfect time to adjust my teaching. Like August, it's a month of fresh starts. Through my work as a literacy coach I have learned the importance of the first six weeks of school. The first weeks of school are sacred weeks: They should go uninterrupted in classrooms everywhere, since it is during this time we get to know one another and build our classroom community together, beginning conversations that will continue as the year progresses.

In my opinion, January is the second most important time of year. In August we looked ahead to the future; but now, in addition to a future, we have a past. Our history together makes it easier to move forward. Since the beginning of the school year we have been weaving conversations together during focus lessons, creating a common language. In addition to our shared dialogue, we now have a collection of books we can revisit and use to sustain the conversations still to come. Over the previous months I have learned about my students. I know their strengths as readers and those areas they have been working on. I know which books they love to sit with during the workshop and which books I am still trying to tempt them to discover. I have taken careful notes about where we have been and can see the road ahead.

Living and Working Together in the Reader's Workshop	Reading for Understanding	Strategies for Independence	Living the Life of a Reader
Assessing Procedures, Routines & Rituals	*Assessing Understanding*	*Assessing Reading Strategies*	*Assessing Decision Making*
• Can students find the materials they need to work?	Is there evidence that students are using comprehension strategies to help with understanding?	What are students doing when the reading is tricky?	What decisions do readers make?
• Can students find places to work?	• Connecting	• What cues are students using to help with their reading? (MSV)	• Are readers choosing books for different reasons?
• Can students participate effectively in the focus lesson, conferences, and share time?	• Predicting	• What cues are they neglecting in their reading?	• Are readers finishing books? (If not, why are they abandoning books?)
• How are readers using their time during the workshop?	• Questioning	• Are students attempting when the reading is tricky?	• Are students spending enough time with just-right books?
• Can students find the books they need to sustain reading?	• Inferring	• Are students monitoring and self-correcting?	• Are students varying the difficulty of their reading?
• Can students read and talk about books with friends?	• Visualizing	• Are students rereading? (If so, when?)	• What genres are students reading?
• Are students keeping book logs that reflect the reading they are doing?	• Determining Importance	• Is the reading phrased and fluent?	• Are readers balancing their reading?
• Are students responding to books appropriately?	• Synthesizing	• What strategies are students are using when the reading is tricky?	• Do students have favorite authors?
	When are students using these strategies?	• Are they flexible in their use of strategies?	• Are readers able to thoughtfully discuss books with a friend?
	How are students using these strategies?	• What do students know about words?	• Are readers setting appropriate reading goals?
	Are they using these strategies in ways that are helpful in making sense of their reading?		
	Are students flexible in their use of strategies?		
	Can students use these strategies in different types of reading?		

It isn't long before we are under way. Students gather on the carpet for our first reading workshop of the new year. What a difference a few weeks can make. Looking at my students, I pause to enjoy the newness this day brings. Noticing several new haircuts, some new outfits, and a few missing teeth, I announce, "You have all learned so much already this school year. Tell me a few things that smart readers do." I am hoping to pull together the threads of the conversations we have been having over the past months. This isn't a new question for the readers in my classroom but one we have been framing our conversations around for months.

"Read a lot," Katie replies quickly.

"Smart readers read a lot," I agree.

"Take their time," Kanna adds.

"What do you mean?" I ask.

"They don't turn the pages fast. They take their time and try to figure out the story," she explains.

"Great thinking. I'd better write these down," I say, as I open my notebook dramatically .

Mason joins the conversation. "They read books about dogs."

"They might read books about dogs. Are you saying that smart readers choose books that are interesting to them?"

"Yes," he agrees.

"Smart readers choose books that are interesting," I say, as I record these words in my notebook. "Like books about dogs?" I look at Mason to see if I have understood him correctly. He nods, and several other kids begin talking over one another to tell about the topics that interest them.

"What else do smart readers do?" I restate the question, trying to get our conversation back on track.

"Smart readers read just-right books," Aaron remarks.

"I'm glad you thought of that," I say to him, writing down his words in my book.

"Is there anything else?" I pause to give everyone time to think.

"Think in their heads," Julio adds.

"Smart readers think in their heads about the story," I repeat, as I jot down his response. "They think about what would make sense or what might happen next. Very smart. Anything else?"

"They go back." Georgia finishes our conversation.

"Smart readers go back and reread when they are stuck," I agree, knowing this is something Georgia was working on before we left for break. "And go back to fix things," I slip in.

This is how I prefer to do assessment in my classroom, in the context of our daily work. I have established routines within the school day that help me document my students' learning. I gather information in conversations like these, during reader's workshop and writer's workshop, and in other learning situations. By listening during read-alouds and shared reading, by attending to our conversations throughout the day, I construct a picture of each reader that informs my decision making. Quick conversations can tell us a lot about what students understand. My day is too short and the school year moves too fast for me to stop my teaching for assessment. Wherever and whenever possible, I weave assessment into the teaching day. As I watch and listen, I look for common threads, while also taking note of individual students who might have specific needs.

In addition to the information I collect throughout the school day, I also find that reflection has helped me to improve the work I do with students. I consider what students show me they know in their reading and writing, the conversations we have had, the books that they have encountered, the curriculum ahead and the insights readers will need. When I look at evidence of children's learning, I first determine what they know about literacy, then what they need to know next. In this way I determine an instructional focus for my class and plan individual support.

In January, the class still needed more time with nonfiction to find out that readers also read to learn, to answer questions, and to discover more. We would need to devote focus lessons to looking at informational text as a class.

In addition, students had reached different places in their reading. I needed to find ways to accommodate them. Kaitlyn needed to learn to monitor her reading and writing. She needed to check her reading visually to be sure that she read the words she saw. She had similar difficulties in writing; she had so much to say, she would try to write it down too quickly and was sometimes careless in recording the sounds she was hearing, so that it was nearly impossible for her to reread her pieces. Sean was starting to read stories with one line of text, relying on repetitive language structures and picture cues. He needed to develop a larger bank of words to help him figure out these stories and monitor his reading. Kierra was learning to talk about the stories she read but needed to work on predicting what was going to happen next. She was still having a hard time telling a story in her writing, and often used her time to draw pictures of houses, flowers, and her family if I didn't get to her early in the writing workshop.

✳ Running Records and Beyond: Tracking Conversations

It is easy to rely only on ear and instinct to determine what young readers understand and need, but my ear and my instinct do not always give me an accurate picture. I have often thought from listening that children are doing one thing, but when I look at their reading on paper I see that they are doing quite another. While sometimes I take formal running records of bench-level texts, most often I take quick, informal running records as I sit beside children and listen to them read. In my notebook I jot down a running record to determine what they are attending to as they read.

Sitting side by side with a child during a conference, listening to the reading while taking a running record, I can combine all the information and consider it in combination with the child's history, body language, confidence, and pace to reflect on the child as a reader. A quick conversation after the reading can help me to note the child's understanding of the story. Then I try to find a way to support this reader. If I have taken a running record, my analysis yields important information. When I analyze a running record, my concern is *not* the level of text the child can read, but *what it is that the child is doing during the reading.* I don't worry so much about whether this was a level 5 book, a level 10 book, and so on, but look to see what information the child is paying attention to, how she helps herself when the reading is tricky, and any patterns I notice in the running record.

I also try to figure out what the child is doing when the reading is challenging. Is the child considering meaning, using picture cues, considering the structure of the sentence, paying attention to visual information? My analysis tells me whether the child is integrating meaning, structure, and visual information in reading, which strategies he is using, and the child's ability to read fluently. If I look carefully I can determine which cues are being used, and which neglected. Using the questions from the assessment chart that determine strategies for independence, I can begin to think about what children have under control and what should be next in their learning. Running records over time trace progress and patterns that lead to responsive teaching decisions.

Running records are only one tool for assessment and work best in determining the strategies novice readers and students making slow progress are using when the reading is tricky. I want to know much more about all of my readers. In addition to running records, I consider other evidence in my assessment. Student reading logs, reader response notebooks, snippets of conversation, books chosen for reading, and conversations with peers all provide me with important insights. (See Figure 7.2.)

※ figure 7.2 Starting Points for Assessment Conversations

Goal of Assessment Conference	Starting Points for Conversation
To determine student understanding of a focus lesson.	• Show me a place in your reading where ...
To determine if a student is able to read for meaning.	• What's happening in your story? • Tell me about what you've read so far. • What have you learned so far? (nonfiction)
To find out about a child's book choices.	• What are you reading? • How is this similar to/different from other books you've read lately? • Why did you choose this book? • What do you plan to read next?
To determine the reading strategies a child is using to read unfamiliar text.	• Will you read this story to me? • Read a page or two to me? • Can I listen to you read starting here?
To hear a child's assessment of his/her own reading progress.	• How's your reading going? • What is working well for you? • What has been difficult? • How can I help you?

When I first began conferring with students, I was so worried about making the right teaching moves, finding the perfect words, and listening to my students that I often forgot to write anything down. Each time I sat down with a child we had a conference that worked for that book at that time but was disconnected from the previous ones. Making myself write down conversations, record quick running records, and note the language children used in my notebook gives me a sense of where we've been and helps me plan where we need to go next.

Finding a way to record and save information has been an ongoing challenge for me. I've used everything from grade books to mailing labels on clipboards to notecards. The system I'm currently using—my favorite so far—is a spiral notebook, tabbed in the back with a section for each student arranged alphabetically. Here I record individual observations, take a short running record, and write down the teaching point.

For each reader, I set aside several pages in which I take notes during literacy activities. I can follow conversations over time and make connections between reading and writing. Jotting down the conference teaching point tells me where I have left off when I return for the next conference.

On the blank pages in the front of the notebook I keep notes about the focus of instruction for each day and jot down students' comments during focus lessons. I sketch out conference plans ahead of time, and, since my students sit in different places each day, plan seating arrangements to optimize my teaching time. My notebook goes with me everywhere during my time in my classroom. I have come to rely on it to such an extent that if I misplace it while I am teaching, I find it hard to continue to teach. I can't seem to think unless it is in my hand. Apparently my students have learned to recognize the lost look on my face, because it always seems that within two minutes, one of my students will say, "Here is your notebook, Mrs. Mere."

※ Learning About Readers in Assessment Conferences

It is Wednesday. My students have come in to find a new Keep Book waiting at their tables. These are small books our P.T.O. has purchased from Ohio State University that children can take home and keep. Students get unpacked and check in. Some head to the media center while others begin to read their new book, *Trucks*. A few students approach me with a grin to tell me they have located *can* and *see* in the text, two of the latest words we have added to our word wall. I hear Brett say to a friend at his table, "This book is about trucks. I have trucks at home that I play with."

Emily is first on my list today. As I kneel beside her, notebook in hand, I ask about the new book. "I can read it," she says with a smile. "I love stories about trucks," I say. "Will you read it to me?" Emily turns to the title page. "Trucks. Trucks. Trucks," she reads giggling. "That's funny, the way they wrote that title over and over, isn't it?" I explained, knowing she had not expected to see the title repeated on the title page. As Emily reads, I take a quick informal running record in my notebook. When she finishes we talk about the story, and I jot a few quick notes. Emily has used meaning and known words to figure out this new story. Her substitution of *toys* for *trucks* also tells me that she is using the beginning letter to help figure out new words, information that she has been working on using independently. I am surprised that she said "toys," since the picture is of trucks and the word *truck* has been used consistently throughout the text. I wonder if she is really using meaning as effectively as I originally thought and make a note to watch carefully.

Students begin to return from the library and I stand up to move to my next conference. Just then Josh comes up with a book in his hand. I can tell by the look on his face that he is very excited about something. "I found an easy book, Mrs. Mere." I glance at the book he is holding, Jillian Cutting's *The Birthday Party*, and am skeptical. Josh has gone from drawing pictures to telling stories in writing workshop. It took several months for him to understand that books tell stories and that our writing does too. His early stories were scribbles, always in green, of "my house," but he is now also using pictures to tell "my dad has a model Hummer." In addition to some improvements in his oral language, he has gone from knowing 14 to knowing 34 of 54 letters on the letter identification assessment but still hasn't shown any sign of using this information to read. He has demonstrated little evidence of a 1:1 match, and his conversations with partners about books still focus on "what is in the picture" and not "what is happening in the story."

Josh isn't on my conference schedule for today, but I always leave enough room to stop when it seems I am needed, and I definitely want to see this. Josh leads me back to his seat. He opens his book and I kneel down beside him. We talk for a bit and he begins to read. "See, that was easy," he states proudly as he closes the book. It's true. Each page contains two words of text, and he has used the known word *the* and the picture to read the story. He has demonstrated a 1:1 match, and while attempts like *food* for *Jell-o* make sense, they are not visually correct. Yet, considering where Josh was as a learner, this is a huge step forward. He'll have time in the weeks to come to discover that *food* doesn't start like that, but he has accomplished two things today: He has found a book he is excited about and he has let me know there is much more I can be doing to support him as a reader.

Glancing over at Rebecca, I notice that she is reading *My Brother* by Joy Cowley. This book about a little brother is far too easy. It is designed for emergent readers: Each page has two words that tell what the little brother is doing. The language is repetitive and the pictures pretty much give the words away. Walking over to Rebecca, I take a deep breath, put on my curious teacher face, and innocently inquire, "Tell me about the book you are reading," resisting the urge to take the book from her hands, hide it on a high shelf, and replace it with one that is a better match for the transitional reader she is. (Thank goodness for self-control!) Rebecca gives me a wide smile, completely unaware of my agenda. "It's a book about a baby brother." Pausing, unsure of my next move, I watch her. "I like it," she adds. "It reminds me of my brother."

Rebecca is a great big sister. Her younger brother is about a year old, and all her writing lately has been about him. "It does remind me a bit of the story you just wrote about your brother," I say. Rebecca is steps ahead of me. She has a purpose for reading this book, and I have nearly destroyed her progress with my leveled thinking (old habits die hard). I want students in my classroom to think beyond levels and have reasons to read. Rebecca had that figured out before she walked into my classroom. "You might want to look through the family basket," I remind her as I come back to my senses. "There are a few more stories over there about brothers that you might enjoy." I point to the basket and make my exit. That was a close one! I make a note to search our library for a few books about brothers that Rebecca might enjoy.

In our school, kindergarten students arrive any time during the first fifteen minutes of the day, and these conferences all take place during that time. This is a great time to have students read independently while everyone else settles in for the day. Students read from a basket of books already on the table. It usually contains a mix of familiar books, books that would be just right for most of the readers in the classroom, and books that, while perhaps a bit challenging, will be interesting to these students. Today the baskets contain many familiar titles from shared reading, a few books that are just right for these novice readers, several versions of *The Three Little Pigs* (our current fairy tale of study), some nonfiction books about birds (our current life science topic of study), and some picture books they have shown an interest in revisiting. They can also read books from their browsing bags during this time.

I value these moments to talk casually with students. My conferences during this part of our day, as I listen and check-in with readers, are usually shorter than those during our workshop. While conferences during the workshop will often end with a teaching point, I usually use this time at the beginning of our day for informal observation and assessment.

In my role as a literacy coach I use these same principles when I assess students in other classrooms. Walking into the first-grade classroom, I begin to watch the children at work. The workshop has already started, and students seem to be settling into their reading. I see books in many areas of the room: math books in baskets in the far corner, nonfiction books on shelves in another corner, and picture books and poetry books lining the front of the room. Students don't have to move far to find a new book. Children are sitting at tables reading by themselves, in pairs, or in threes. Some are reading in pockets of space carefully created by the teacher all around her classroom.

Watching them at work I soon notice Alex, who is up and wandering around the room throughout the workshop. He is a social butterfly, disrupting pairs wherever he goes and drawing others into conversations that are not about books. I finally decide to go talk with him to see how his reading is going. I have already seen his inattention but want to hear him talk about his activities. He is quick to respond to my questions about his book. "What else have you read today?" I ask. He fumbles for words, trying to assemble a reading record for the day.

When I talk to his teacher later, she confirms my suspicions. This is a typical day for Alex. He is able to read many books, but he does just what is required of him to get by. He hasn't developed an interest in reading. His teacher feels that he is not working up to his potential and is difficult to motivate. We need to find ways to help Alex engage in reading while acknowledging his social nature. Perhaps finding a reading buddy for him and developing a reading plan would be a place to start.

I used to feel guilty about not conferring or working with students the entire time that was available, but I now use some time simply to watch. When I send students off to read, I keep an eye out to see how long it takes them to get started. Who has a hard time settling down? Who seems to have difficulty staying with their reading? I pay attention to what students are reading and the friends they seem to enjoy reading together with each day. I watch to see if students can find the books they need and comfortable places in which to read.

I also listen to students in conversations with peers, in whole-class conversations, in small-group discussions, and in conferences. Third graders Austin and Shane, reading a book from the *Horrible Harry* series by Suzy Kline together, demonstrated some of the ways students can support one another in their reading. These two boys read together almost seamlessly. They took turns reading softly, the other following along. When one reader had difficulty, the other would help out by supplying a word, explaining the meaning, or asking questions. They were each equally in charge of the text. As we gathered at the end of the workshop I asked the boys to model the work they had been doing for the rest of the class. These reading partnerships provide an incentive to read and offer additional support to readers.

Since I have made more time in the day for assessment conferences, I find that I am enjoying my teaching, and my students, more than ever. These conferences are an essential tool in getting to know readers in my classroom at the beginning of the year and paying attention to their progress, and in finding out about the readers in the classrooms where I coach.

CHAPTER 8

Finding Balance

As a teacher, I have had to teach myself a few things over the years. First, I've had to learn that reading is not always a problem. This has actually been very liberating. For so long, I looked at reading instruction as if I were a firefighter, running here and there putting out fires; everything was a near emergency that needed my immediate attention. Now I think of myself more as a sculptor gradually shaping a new work. In fact, more often than not, reading is anything but a problem. Students work through long periods of time without difficulty, and many progress smoothly. My goal for readers has moved beyond helping them to reach the next benchmark book to helping them see the vast reading possibilities beyond our classroom.

Second, I have learned to remind myself that in my classroom teaching and learning happen all day. My teaching does not happen only in guided reading. If I haven't met with a child in a guided reading group, it doesn't mean that I haven't taught that child. My teaching begins during the focus lesson, where children participate in conversations that develop their thinking. I can guide individual readers during a read-aloud or shared reading by tailoring my questions and conversation to their specific needs. During a read-aloud, I might stop to help Tamarah retell what has just happened in the book we are reading to help her think about the story. I might ask Kanna why she thought a character made a particular decision to help her to make inferences about the character's actions. I might ask Nazarena what she thinks will happen before I turn the page to help her begin to do what I know she must learn to do in her own reading. These decisions don't take tons of planning, just thoughtful attention to my students as we talk together about stories. During interactive writing, word study, and independent writing I can help students to see how words work. These insights support not only these studies but also the reading they do. The reality is that I now do a much better job meeting the needs of my students. I spend more time talking with them individually, more time observing them as they read, more time reflecting on their responses, more time shaping instruction to connect everything they do throughout the day.

Billy, a Spanish-speaking student, joined us a week after school began. He did not utter a word of English for weeks, and I wasn't sure how much he actually understood. During read-alouds he had a difficult time listening. Sometimes I'd glance up from the book and see him turned around smiling at the student behind him. Sometimes, as the other students waited eagerly to see what would happen when I turned the page, he'd get up and walk to the drinking fountain, totally unaware of our excitement. To him, in those early days, I must have sounded a bit like Charlie Brown's teacher, "WAH, WAH, WAH."

His ELL teacher, Dawn Davenport, told me that if I used a few Spanish words for key vocabulary in the story it would help him begin to understand. If a read-aloud was going to be the focus of our conversation over several days, she'd often read it with Billy first, taking the time to use some Spanish vocabulary and to talk with him about the story. Neither one of us spoke any Spanish, but we'd managed to learn a few key words with the help of Spanish dictionaries and knowledgeable Spanish-speaking students. Dawn was always better at learning new vocabulary than I was, and my struggles constantly reminded me of how challenging it must be for Billy to learn in our classroom each day. Our efforts started to show results during read-alouds.

Billy was actually like many kindergarten students; he needed language before he would be able to make effective use of reading strategies. After he learned to tell stories about his own experience during writer's workshop, we were able to continue to build on his language. At first he'd point and name things in Spanish, and we'd try to provide the English. Later he began telling stories in short English phrases. He wrote most often about playing with friends or topics from read-alouds, or he would retell familiar stories. As Billy started to learn to read, I began to look for books with simple phrases, repetitive text, strong picture support, and concepts that were similar to those he wrote about most often.

My classroom is about my students. I seek to balance our activities in ways that will support them as lifelong readers and writers.

✳ Guided Reading As Part of the Mix

Supporting readers means crafting the instruction I provide to students. When planning instruction, I first consider what my focus will be: What do I want students to know or understand? After I have planned the lesson I determine which students might need more support with this new strategy or concept than I can provide in the whole-group focus lesson and which students might need some other type of support to make continued progress. If I have a few students with similar needs, I group them together. The rest I plan to meet with in conferences throughout the week.

Sitting down with Colleen Csiszarik, a second-grade teacher, I see that she has a grid of fifteen reading time slots which, I can tell by the change in pen color, has recently grown from ten. Also in front of her are seven cards with the names of her twenty-seven students divided among them into groups. "I just can't get it to work out," she says in frustration. "Let's consider what your kids really need right now," I suggest, trying to focus the conversation on students' needs. "You have to remember that your kids are not reading only in guided-reading groups." When we were using guided reading for most of our reading instruction, students were not spending as much time reading in the classroom as they do now.

Students in her classroom spend time each day reading independently while she confers with individual students and meets with small groups. "You also have to remember that you are not teaching only during guided reading. For example, your focus lesson today was about predicting. Watching and listening to your students today, I would say that most of them understand how to predict what is next in a story and will be able to use that strategy in their reading. You are also teaching during your focus lesson and when you listen to students."

We looked at the groups she had listed on the cards in front of us and began to talk about the best ways to help these readers. We began with Jose, Bree, and David, three readers receiving either Title or ELL services. These readers were beginning to be more flexible in their use of strategies to read unfamiliar text, but they were still behind their peers. They had made gains this year, but we wanted to accelerate their progress. Since these three readers had similar needs, we decided that it made sense to meet with them together.

The second group we discussed consisted of six students: Kaitlyn, Danielle, Julio, Evan, Sandra, and Dani. All six seemed to need a lift in their independent reading. They understood predicting but needed to be more engaged in the reading they were doing. We decided to pull them aside to get a better picture of how they were thinking about their reading. We would have this group read and record their questions. We would work together on the first few pages of the story, and when it seemed that everyone understood the task, we'd have students continue to read the story independently. The questions students recorded and our conversation together should provide some insight into their thinking. We'd also be introducing another strategy they could use to make sense of text.

It would make sense to meet with the other students during conferences to check on their progress, provide specific teaching, and continue the conversations of the focus lesson. Colleen was still concerned about Alyssa and Kassie. Both of these readers received support outside the classroom, and both were reading considerably below grade level. She had originally planned to meet with them together, but as we talked, it became apparent that their needs were too different. Colleen decided that she would meet with these two readers individually for a short time each day to check-in, introduce new books, or monitor familiar reading.

The conversations I have with teachers about guided reading are more often about managing small-group instruction than about its effectiveness. I am often asked, "How many groups should I meet with each day?" "How do I put these lowest five readers together when the strategies they use vary so greatly or the complexity of text they can read is so different?" "My students are in groups with like needs, but I have seven groups. I want to put students in five groups so that I can fit everyone into my schedule. Can you come help me combine my groups together?" These questions arise, I believe, precisely because we know that our students don't always fit neatly into groups, that time constraints make it challenging to meet with all students in groups, that some students need more intensive support, that some needs are better met during other parts of the day, and that some students don't really need the additional support of small-group instruction at this time, but we feel guilty. If we are not meeting with each of our students in a guided-reading group, we must not be doing any teaching.

I too used to look at all the students, find common areas that children needed to work on in their reading, and place them—all of them—in groups of four to six readers. Of course there was always the issue of text level, and often in the interest of time I had to form guided-reading groups in which children similar in level needed very different strategic support, or place readers in groups where the reading was either a bit too easy or too challenging. I felt that if I didn't have students in groups all the time I surely couldn't be meeting their needs. I used to worry, but then I realized—or finally admitted to myself—that the students in my classroom did not always fit into groups, nor did they always need this level of support. I quit trying to find ways to fit everyone into a group and started to consider the needs of my readers.

✳ Making Guided Reading an Effective Instructional Tool

If through assessments, conferences, and observations I have noticed a group of readers who need similar instruction, or if a small group will need more support than the focus lesson, I may bring them together. It is really an issue of time management. If I am going to have conferences with several students to provide the exact same support, why not group them together?

When I notice a group of students who need the same type of support, I may bring them together for a short time. For example, during conferences I noticed that Ahmad, Roger, Andrew, and Andy were able to read text using known words, but as the text's difficulty increased they were all having a hard time reading because they were not using meaning to attempt to predict an unknown word. Since all four needed the same type of instruction, I decided to put them together for small-group instruction. We met during the workshop in a guided-reading group that focused on rereading difficult text and thinking about the meaning of the story when encountering new words. I knew they would soon need to utilize the beginning letter in the word, but first they needed to learn to attempt the word independently and monitor these attempts in their reading.

I met with the four boys for about three days. After that, they returned to the workshop to use this new strategy in their reading. I monitored them carefully in conferences to be sure that they had taken on this strategy and provided additional support as needed. Three days was enough time to put the strategy in place and to hold them accountable for it in their reading.

Working with readers in a small group makes sense when

- Students need additional support with concepts from the focus lesson
- Students need the focus lesson to be extended
- Students need specific support that may be different from the focus lesson
- It is helpful to check-in quickly with readers about a specific concept, strategy, or understanding
- Small group conversations will aid readers' understanding

To make guided reading more effective, I choose students for groups carefully. I may use guided reading if I have noticed:

- *Readers who need help learning to think about their reading.* These readers need to learn to read for understanding. I asked a group of first graders to cover up the titles of a few easy stories. After we had read them, we talked together about the titles we might choose. This conversation helped us to think about the main message the author wanted us to take away from the text. Students might also require help learning to consider their prior knowledge, ask questions, make inferences, visualize the story, determine importance, or synthesize information. These students may need to learn to return to the text to support their responses or apply the strategies they used for one genre to a different genre.

- *Readers who need support learning to use every cue in reading.* These children come together briefly because they are all ignoring the same information. For example, over-relying on visual information can make it difficult to read for understanding. If a group of readers are stopping to sound out words and ignoring the meaning of the story, I would put this group together to remind them of the importance of thinking about the story. Thinking about the story can allow readers to tackle unfamiliar words.

- *Readers who need to monitor their reading and self-correct.* These readers need to monitor their reading to be sure that it makes sense and looks right. I might group students together because they are saying the words regardless of whether the reading looks right or makes sense. Groups might be brought together to work on monitoring their understanding of chapter books or nonfiction. With a group of second-grade students reading chapter books for understanding, I talked about stopping at the end of each chapter to make sure they understood what had happened. Teaching readers to stop and think helps them monitor their reading.

- *Readers who need to learn to consider cues more carefully during reading.* Four first-grade readers making good progress in their reading were having the same difficulty. They were using meaning, structure, and visual information to read new text, but they were not sampling enough visual information on their first attempt to read unfamiliar words. The books they were now reading required them to look beyond the first letter and search through the word. These readers needed support to learn to search for more visual information.

- *Readers who need support as they learn to read books in unfamiliar series or genres.* A group of second-grade students, beginning to read the "Nate the Great" series, needed help in understanding the structure of a mystery. Mysteries tend to work backwards: first the problem, then the clues that help solve the case. We worked together to become familiar with the characters, learn about the structure of these books, and notice clues. Drawing on what students already know to understand how the story works would support future reading of books in this series.

■ *Readers who need to make accelerated progress to catch up with peers.* These children often need explicit and systematic teaching. In my classroom I find my struggling readers immediately and meet with them in some way every day. If it is difficult to meet with them individually every day, and the support provided in whole-group lessons is not specific enough to their needs, I find small-group instruction an effective way to keep them moving.

❊ Making the Most of Guided Reading

I've learned to be more intentional in my teaching during guided-reading lessons (see Figure 8.1). When students do meet in a guided-reading group, I want the instruction to be effective. Most lessons still begin with an introduction, then students read, and then there is some follow-up discussion. I've found ways to adapt parts of this process to achieve quick shifts in learning. I begin by making sure my instruction has a focus. When I used to give guided reading lessons my goal was to have students move through levels of increasingly challenging text, but my teaching point was most often a result of difficulty in the story. Now I try to lead with the teaching point to guide our conversation during the lesson from beginning to end.

Familiar Reading

Students bring their browsing bag of familiar books when I call them for guided reading. They start to read as they wait for other students to join us and get settled, which allows me to listen to readers before we begin, checking reading strategies, listening for fluency, and engaging in short discussions about the stories students are reading. Familiar reading is especially important for novice readers, readers striving to make progress, second-language readers, and readers working to improve fluency.

Brittany, Torii, Korall, Austin, and Cory bring their browsing bags to the carpet, where I have asked them to join me. Korall arrives first, pulls a familiar book out of her bag, and begins to read. Other students do the same as we wait for the group to get settled. I've brought these readers together to follow up on the focus

✳ figure 8.1   **Making the Most of Guided Reading**

Planning
- Place students together in a small group *only* if they need the same type of support
- Know exactly what you want children to know
- Choose a book that will support the teaching
- Read the book and determine the supports and challenges within the text
- Plan an introduction that will meet the needs of the readers
- Plan language that will help students to take on this new strategy or understanding
- Know how you will assess student understanding of this new strategy

Before
- Tell students the reason you brought them all together
- Demonstrate the new strategy or discuss the new understanding
- Tailor your introduction to meet the needs of your readers

During
- Begin by telling students exactly what it is you want them to do
- Ask all students to read the text (silently or aloud)
- Stay focused on the new learning
- Use clear language to prompt and praise readers during the reading
- Keep lessons short and to the point

After
- Talk about the story after it has been read
- Return to the text to locate evidence to support responses
- Discuss or go back to the places where the new strategy was used
- Connect new strategy or understanding to the reading students are doing in the workshop

In the days that follow
- Allow time for independent practice (do not teach something new the very next day)
- Be sure students are reading books that will allow them to practice this new strategy
- Check in with students during conferences to monitor progress
- Hold students accountable for this new strategy

lesson demonstrating the ways we balance meaning and visual information in our reading. I listen in to see how well these readers are using meaning to read their stories. These five readers, in this case all at a similar stage in their reading, need to balance meaning with visual information. On their first attempt they do not balance all cues, but instead consider visual information first. Of greater concern is that they often keep on reading, without going back after the miscue. To get them to use meaning on their first attempt, I want to get them to pay attention to the place where they ignored meaning and go back to fix their reading, reinforcing the point that reading has to make sense.

The Teaching Point

I used to start the guided reading with an introduction and then have students read, waiting until they finished to make my teaching point, which was usually determined by students' difficulties with the book. This approach produced inconsistent lessons that focused more on reading particular books than on strategies that could be used in all reading and would be most beneficial to particular readers. Because different books often led to different complications, I was making a new teaching point each day, which was especially problematic for struggling readers. Instead of waiting until the end of a story to determine a teaching point, I have found it more effective to know my teaching point when I first begin to work with students, beginning the lesson by telling them what I have noticed in their reading that has made me bring them together. Now, instead of waiting until the end of the lesson I start with this point and weave it throughout our time together. I tell students what I have noticed about their reading, demonstrate strategies or discuss understandings that may be helpful, and have students give it a try.

Looking at the group I begin, "I have noticed that when you are reading and you are unsure of a word, you guess something that starts with that letter, but it doesn't always make sense. Today when you are reading, if you notice that your reading doesn't make sense, I want you to go back and fix it. Try something that looks right and *makes sense*."

The Introduction

In determining the appropriate amount of support for an introduction I consider the experience of the reader, the difficulty of the text, and the strategy I want to teach. As I plan the introduction, I take into account the challenges that the text may hold for readers. Moving in and out of class-rooms I have discovered favorite books I like to use for guided-reading lessons. Despite the fact that I have used some books many times, I find that my introduction is different in each lesson, since I tailor it to meet the needs of those particular students.

For this group I chose the book *Baby Bear Goes Fishing* by Beverley Randell, which has a typical beginning-middle-end story structure. These students have read other stories about Baby Bear and his family, so they have some background knowledge that may also help support their reading.

Before passing out the books I begin my introduction, telling students about the story. "In this story, Baby Bear wants to go fishing with Father Bear, but Father Bear thinks Baby Bear is too little. Mother Bear talks Father Bear into taking Baby Bear fishing. They go down to the river to fish, but the fish are not appearing. Father Bear can't catch any fish. You'll never guess who catches the fish they'll have for dinner!" This is a supportive introduction because I want students to be successful using meaning as they read.

Book Introductions:
- set children up to read
- tell children about story
- go over important features of the plot
- capture student attention
- introduce the characters' names
- introduce tricky language structures or difficult vocabulary
- discuss unfamiliar concepts
- help children construct meaning from the pictures
- provide an opportunity to connect the story to students' lives
- help children make predictions about the story
- allow opportunities for reading work
- flexibly adjust the lesson to meet the needs of the readers.

Everyone Reads

Students keep their books closed until I ask them to begin. In guided-reading groups, where students are going to read aloud, I stagger the children, providing an opportunity for each child to read the complete text, but keeping her from listening in to the reader beside her. Because they are in the early stages of reading and I want to hear their attempts to use the new strategy, all students read aloud. If two students sitting beside one another end up in the same place, I begin talking to one about the story to slow him down, move another away from the group a bit, stop one of the readers, or send someone back to the beginning of the page. Each child reads the entire story.

Moving around the group, I take notes, record the reading of bits of text, prompt students to use the new strategy when appropriate, and praise attempts to use the new strategy during the reading. "Did that make sense?" I ask Cory as he turns the page. "I like the way you went back to make your reading make sense," I say to Brittany as she completes a page of her story after rereading to self-correct. I try to focus my attention on one reader at a time, dividing my time among the members of the group. While my attention is on one reader, my ear is alert for readers who have difficulty with text and may need support and for opportunities to reinforce the teaching of this new strategy.

Reinforcing the Teaching Point

We close the lesson by talking about the story. Students are not surprised that Baby Bear is the one to have caught the fish for dinner. They talk about being told they were too little to do something that they were able to do. Our discussion isn't long, just enough to make sure that everyone has an understanding of the events of the story and that everyone has a chance to share his or her thinking.

To reinforce the teaching point, I have students return to a place where they noticed that their reading didn't make sense and they went back to fix it. As students go back out into the workshop for independent reading I remind them, "Today as you read, if you notice that something doesn't make sense, go back and try to fix it. Reading has to make sense." This group returns to the workshop to read, with today's lessons setting them up for success.

⋰ Selecting Texts for Guided Instruction

An important part of making a guided-reading lesson an effective context for learning is finding a book that offers the appropriate supports and challenges. If I am meeting with children to teach them to match their finger to print as they read, I select a book in which there is only one line of text and a few known words they can use as anchors. If I am teaching children to monitor visual information, I choose a book in which the meaning is supported by the text and the pictures, but whose words might not be the first word a child would predict. If I am teaching children to use meaning, I choose a book with a story structure that supports their understanding or a topic they already have some prior knowledge of so they can read for meaning. If I am teaching early fluency, I choose a book on the easier side with the text laid out in phrases, and repetitive language or dialogue. If I am teaching students how to find the main idea, I choose a short piece with a clear message.

We are fortunate to have a bookroom in our school that houses multiple copies of titles for guided reading. These books, arranged alphabetically by title and sorted by guided-reading levels (Fountas and Pinnell 1996), support guided reading in our classrooms. Books are very generally grouped according to common characteristics, supports, and challenges, the better to match readers to books. Leveled libraries simplify the complexity of choosing books for small groups.

However, some caution is necessary. Leveled libraries can guide teachers, but teachers need to know their readers. I have witnessed teachers throwing their hands up in frustration after a guided-reading lesson flopped because "level E" readers were unable to read a "level E" book successfully. Knowing readers and checking books before a lesson to determine the demands they will make on students can improve success with book choices.

I also consider the length of the piece when choosing texts for guided reading. Short texts can be powerful support for readers. Magazine articles, poems, *Write Time for Kids*, and similar short texts can provide opportunities to demonstrate and practice new strategies, develop thinking, and allow for engaging conversations. Teaching points are often better illustrated in short, explicit instruction.

When choosing books for guided reading, I consider

- *Interest:* I find that guided-reading lessons and conversations go better if students connect to the book. Books on interesting topics that tell about events similar to those occurring in children's lives and containing familiar characters have wide appeal.

- *Topic:* The more previous experience students have with a topic, the more likely a book on that topic will succeed in guided reading. I have seen books bomb because they are about places or events students outside children's experience. I can sometimes provide some background through a strong introduction, but reading is easier when readers have some familiarity with a topic and its vocabulary.

- *Text placement and arrangement:* I also consider page design: where the text is placed on the page and how it is arranged. Beginning readers need consistency. As they make progress, they learn to manage print wherever it appears on the page. Well-designed pages can support work with phrasing and fluency and be important when children read for information in nonfiction texts.

- *Picture support:* In first books I look for pictures. Obviously, the simpler the pictures, the more likely the reader will use them as cues in reading.

Illustrations continue to support reading progress because added details make the match between words and pictures more challenging. Eventually the story itself provides enough information, and pictures play a smaller role.

- *Book language:* Repetitive language encourages novice readers, but as they progress, language can become more challenging. Although some readers are familiar with "once upon a time" or "happily ever after," the language structure in some books can be confusing. Attention to language prepares readers for the challenges that may accompany new text.

- *Story structure:* Does the story move from first to next to last? Are there flashbacks? Is the story cumulative? Story structure affects understanding. In choosing books for guided reading, teachers should consider whether the structure of the story will be familiar or challenging.

- *Vocabulary:* Are there unfamiliar words or phrases in the story? A book introduction can introduce new vocabulary. At the same time, too many unknown words can interfere with understanding.

⟡ Teaching with Intention in Guided Reading

A clear sense of purpose and focus make guided reading more effective. Consider the prompts in the following two lessons. In the first, the teacher has chosen a "level H" book for a group of "level H" readers. The book tells a cumulative story about the noises heard in the city. During the lesson the teacher gives students the following prompts:

- go back and read
- think about the story
- how did that word begin
- try something
- look at the picture
- go back to the beginning of the sentence
- what happens when two vowels are together
- what do we call that (teacher points to the classroom ceiling)
- what do *c* and *h* say when they are together

In the second lesson, the teacher realizes that students are becoming more flexible in how they figure out new words. Students reread and use visual information, usually attending only to the beginning letter. The vocabulary in their books is getting more challenging, however, so the first letter is often not enough. The teacher thinks that if they use the first three or four letters, they might make more accurate attempts. She chooses a book with a typical beginning-middle-end structure to allow them to pay more attention to visual information. During this lesson the teacher uses the following prompts:

- let's look at the first three letters and think about what would make sense
- let's try to put these first four letters together
- let's try it together (she covers the word except for the first letters and together they reread this larger chunk)
- I like the way you put those together

In the second lesson, students' attention is focused on information they have been neglecting in their reading. This teacher uses prompts that will support them as they try this new strategy. This lesson will carry beyond this book to all their future reading.

If I notice something students need to learn to do, I want them to learn to do it. I keep my lesson focused on this point. First graders Emma, Jacob, Jason, Sydney, and Jonathon were reading books with more complicated story lines, often with four to eight lines of text that required a more flexible use of reading strategies. These readers had learned to reread to help themselves figure out unknown words, but sometimes they would reread several times and still be stumped. I wanted to show them another approach.

When I meet with a group of students I have concrete reasons for the decisions I make. Before these readers gathered at the table I had determined the focus of my instruction, planned what I would say to support our conversation, and considered prompts that might be helpful. Once the students were seated at the table I pulled out our book for the lesson, *Sloppy Tiger and the Party* by Joy Cowley. The kids had read and enjoyed other stories about Sloppy Tiger. I knew their familiarity with this character and the problems he caused would help them read this story for understanding.

First I remind students of what they already know; then I tell them I have noticed a sticking point and demonstrate a new strategy I think will be helpful. "When you come to a word you don't know, you often reread to figure it out," I said to my group of first graders. "That works well for all of you, but sometimes these tricky parts are early in the sentence or paragraph and rereading doesn't give you enough information. Today I am going to show you another strategy that might help you to read more challenging books: If you come to a tricky place in your reading, go ahead and reread if you need to, but then try a word and read on." I used to have students skip the word and then come back, but I have found that the word they try is often right, and if not, it is easy to go back because they have gained a bit of information about the structure of the sentence. I give a brief introduction to the book and remind students again of the new strategy: "When you come to a tricky part, try it and read on."

As these students read I listened for opportunities to reinforce the day's lesson. After a few pages Jason attempted a word, but realized as he read on that it didn't make sense, so he reread to self-correct. "That worked well for you. Do you see the way you tried something and when you read on you noticed it didn't make sense? You were able to go back and fix it," I said as he finished the page. The other readers just needed a prompt: "Try it."

"Try it" was not enough support for Emma. When Emma noticed that she needed more information to figure out a word, she would reread but then she would stop. I tried a more supportive prompt: "Go back again and try something that makes sense and looks right." Still she seemed hesitant so I reread with her, lowering my voice as we came to the unknown word. Emma was going to need more help learning to use this strategy in her reading.

In small groups students make the greatest gains if I stay focused. I am careful not to confuse readers by trying to cover several different points. Demonstrating the strategy, praising attempts to use the strategy, and using explicit language in guided reading helps me to keep the lesson short. I want students to leave the lesson with the language that will help them as they use this new strategy in their independent reading. I met with these readers several more times, keeping the focus of teaching the same, to help them to secure this new strategy.

Small-Group Conversations

In addition to using guided reading to help students to learn new strategies, small-group instruction is also a good place to support conversations about books. Sometimes we get so caught up in teaching primary students how to read, especially young students, that we forget to support their thinking. Talking together in a small-group context can help readers learn to connect reading to their lives, discover new ways to discuss books, go back to the text to support their responses, and think critically about what they are reading.

Some students in our primary classrooms need more help thinking about books. Mitchell, a first grader, has been the topic of many of our literacy team meetings. He began his first-grade year receiving small-group intervention because he was reading below grade level. It didn't take long for Mitchell to learn to read words, but thinking about the story remained a challenge for him. When we looked at Mitchell's midyear progress, he was "reading" well above many of his peers in the intervention program, but he was still unable to comprehend what he was reading. We wrestled with how best to meet his needs and decided he should remain in our intervention program.

He would need guided conversations about books to learn how to think about his reading. We would teach him some explicit strategies to encourage comprehension and show him how to go back to the text to answer questions and make sense of his reading. Looking at guided reading as a way to support readers working to make progress may remind us to apply this structured approach more flexibly. Small-group conversations can help readers like Mitchell become members of our reading communities.

By broadening our definition of guided instruction we can support readers like Sierra who continue to need support across years to develop as readers. Walking into the fourth-grade classroom, I spotted Sierra sitting on the floor near her teacher, notebook in hand. It had been two years since I had last seen her. She was a bit taller and her hair was a bit shorter, but otherwise she looked much the same. I had last worked with Sierra in second grade as she had struggled to keep up with her peers in reading. I had enjoyed our time together during that year. Sierra had wanted to be successful, wanted to understand the books she read, but it hadn't been easy for her. She returned to our school as a fourth grader after spending her third-grade year in a nearby school system.

Her teacher, Melissa Mominey, requested that I come in and observe Sierra and two other classmates because she was concerned about their progress. As students gathered on the carpet for the read-aloud, I found a seat near Sierra so that I would be able not only to hear her responses but to see the writing in her notebook. Melissa retold the conversations they had been having about using inference during reading. She pulled out a book by Eve Bunting, *On Call Back Mountain*, and began to read. The class had been talking for several days about inferring and she asked students to write down the inferences they had made during the story. Sierra drew a line down the middle of her page, signaling she was ready to give this a try. "Dylan," Melissa said, "tell me one thing about inferring." Dylan paused, thought for a moment, and replied, "I am inferring that David is happy about getting a green ticket in gym today."

It was obvious from watching and listening to Sierra that she was having a hard time using inference as a reading strategy. After the story Melissa came to me and said, "You see why I am so worried." I agreed that there were things about Sierra that concerned me, but I still saw in her the qualities that I loved the first time I worked with her. She was still working hard to be successful. She was still trying to make sense of the stories she was hearing and reading.

Sierra did have a lot of work ahead of her, but I could see the hurdles she had jumped since second grade. "The good thing about Sierra," I said to Melissa, "is that she knows when she doesn't understand. She is trying to make sense of stories, and she's asking questions." This was a big step forward for her. "She knows when she is confused and the more we can get her to articulate her confusion the more we can provide the support she needs to move forward."

We talked about the ways Sierra could be supported in the classroom. Sierra needed conversations like the one today during the read-aloud. She needed to work to make sense of stories with the help of other experienced readers. She needed to learn to go back to the text to support her thinking. It would take many conversations to help her in reading increasingly challenging text. We would support her during conversations in other contexts, but our focus needed to stay on reading for understanding. We thought it would be best for Sierra to have these conversations in a conference or in a small group to give her more opportunities to respond.

Readers like Sierra have often learned to "break the code," but continue to have difficulty reading for understanding. As we talked about Sierra, we realized that learning to infer was going to be a challenge. As she tried to make sense of the story her attention seemed drawn to unimportant details. She easily went off track in her reading. We thought bringing her back to asking questions would lead into inferring, but the small-group lesson was not successful. She didn't have enough information about what she was reading to ask questions that moved her forward in the text.

We needed to step back even more to help Sierra as a reader. She was trying to read chapter books during independent reading, but these longer stories were even more challenging. Using picture books to teach Sierra some strategies for reading would be a good place to start, and later we could connect this learning to the reading she was doing in chapter books and in other content areas.

Seth and Allen also needed help in reading for understanding, so we decided to bring the three of them together. Choosing the picture book, *The Gift Stone* by Robyn Eversole, I went through the story and stuck lined sticky notes at what seemed to be natural breaks. I knew that life on an opal farm would be unfamiliar to them but planned to clear this up a bit with my introduction. I knew they would understand the struggles of this family.

Sierra smiles as she comes to the table. Seth rolls his eyes and I can almost hear his thoughts ("Here comes that reading teacher again to make me work. You can't make me work today"), as he approaches the table. After breaking the ice with a bit of conversation I begin, "Have you ever been reading and suddenly realized that you have no idea what you have just read? Sometimes I will be reading and get to the end of a chapter and have no idea what happened in the chapter, so I have to go back and read it again." Sierra says this very thing has happened to her, but Seth and Allen can't remember it happening to them, which concerns me even more.

"Readers stop and think as they read to make sure that they understand the author's message," I tell them as I introduce this book. "This is a story about a girl named Jean. Her family doesn't have much money, so they move to an opal farm to find work. On the opal farm they search for stones that are used for jewelry. Let's see what we can learn about Jean's life," and I show them a picture inside the book. I keep my introduction short. If I give the story away before we begin, I will not be able to learn more about them as readers.

We read the first few sections together, pausing to reflect before writing down our response. I want to be sure everyone knows what to do and understands enough about the story to begin to work independently. I ask them to stop at the end of each section as they read silently and wait to go on with the story. I want them to have a conversation with each other that will help them to know if they understand what they are reading.

We discuss the story as we move through sections, and something inspires Seth to begin to write questions on the blue question sticky notes I have brought along. It is not long before they are all writing a short statement about what has happened in the section and jotting down questions. They are all sitting tall in their seats now, and my role as leader of the conversation is slowly turning to that of a guide.

Seth is on a roll now, summarizing sections and asking questions as he moves through the story. Sierra is also making progress. The fact that they are now asking questions as they read is helping me to see what they understand. Because they are working at different rates it is easy to talk to them about their thinking individually before they move on. I'm a bit concerned about Allen. He is taking longer to read the story and seems to need to articulate his thoughts before writing them down.

We stop reading just as Jean finds something behind the refrigerator. "What did she find?" Allen asks. I nearly blurt out the word *opal*, but something stops me. I know from their written responses that Sierra and Seth have figured out that it is an opal, and to me it seems so obvious I am certain when I go back to reread I'll find the word *opal* right on the page. But it isn't there. The author doesn't come out and say Jean found an opal. "Why don't you ask Sierra and Seth," I advise Allen, trying to keep the conversation among the three of them. Sierra and Seth refer to the text to explain their thinking and we continue.

As we finish the story Sierra reads her question to Seth and Allen: "Why did Jean want to live with her grandparents?" The students try to explain their thoughts, referring back to the text and drawing on their own experience. This lesson ends as students infer the answer. We have come full circle in this guided conversation. "What did you learn about yourselves as readers?" I ask before we stop. Sierra tells us that it has helped to stop and think as she reads to make sense of the story, and Seth agrees. Allen reminds us that it helped him to go back and reread when the story didn't make sense.

These conversations will continue for these readers as they learn to look deeply into the stories they are reading. This same strategy will carry over to content-area reading and chapter books. Conversations are powerful ways to help students make sense of their reading, but one conversation does not magically improve readers. Sierra is a perfect example of a reader who needs time to develop.

If our schools looked beyond the pressure and short-term goals of testing and standards to encouraging life-long readers, our classrooms might look different yet still accomplish these goals. Reading makes readers.

Allington, Richard L. 2001. *What Really Matters for Struggling Readers.* New York: Addison-Wesley Longman.

Angelillo, Janet. 2003. *Writing About Reading.* Portsmouth, NH: Heinemann.

Bacon, Ron. 1988. *Our Dog Sam.* Mt. Eden, Auckland: Shortland Publications.

Banks, Kate. 1996. *Spider, Spider.* New York: Farrar, Straus and Giroux.

Barton, Byron. 1991. *The Three Bears.* New York: HarperCollins.

Blume, Judy. 1984. *The Pain and the Great One.* New York: Dell.

Bourgeois, Paulette. 1995. *Franklin Wants a Pet.* New York: Scholastic.

Bulla, Dale. 1995. *My Brother's a Pain in the Back Seat.* Carrollton, TX: New Horizon Press.

Bunting, Eve. 1997. *On Call Back Mountain.* New York: Blue Sky Press.

Burningham, John. 1978. *Would You Rather...* New York: Crowell.

Calkins, Lucy McCormick. 2001. *The Art of Teaching Reading.* New York: Addison-Wesley Educational Publishers.

Carle, Eric. 1990. *The Very Quiet Cricket.* New York: Philomel Books.

———. 1997. *From Head to Toe.* New York: HarperCollins.

Clay, Marie. 1991. *Becoming Literate.* Portsmouth, NH: Heinemann.

Collins, Kathy. 2004. *Growing Readers: Units of Study in the Primary Classroom.* Portland, ME: Stenhouse Publishers.

Cowley, Joy. 1986. *Huggles' Breakfast.* Bothell, WA: The Wright Group.

————. 1989. *Sloppy Tiger and the Party.* Bothell, WA: The Wright Group.

————. 1990. *The Hungry Giant.* Bothell, WA: The Wright Group.

————. 1993. *Wishy-Washy Day.* Bothell, WA: The Wright Group.

————. 1998. *Do Not Open This Book.* Bothell, WA: The Wright Group.

Crews, Donald. 1985. *The Bicycle Race.* New York: Greenwillow Books.

Cronin, Doreen. 2001. *Click, Clack, Moo: Cows That Type.* New York: Simon & Schuster.

Cullinan, Bernice. 1996. *A Jar of Tiny Stars.* Honesdale, PA: Wordsong, Boyds Mills Press.

Cutting, Jillian. 1988. *The Birthday Party.* San Diego: The Wright Group.

Day, Alexandra. 1998. *Follow Carl!* New York: Farrar, Straus and Giroux.

de Paola, Tomie. 1979. *Oliver Button Is a Sissy.* San Diego: Harcourt Brace Jovanovich.

Ehlert, Lois. 1987. *Growing Vegetable Soup.* San Diego: Harcourt Brace Jovanovich.

Emberley, Ed. 1992. *Go Away, Big Green Monster.* Boston: Little, Brown.

Evans, Lynette. 1997. *The Little Snowman.* Crystal Lake, IL: Rigby.

Eversole, Robyn. 1998. *The Gift Stone.* New York: Knopf.

Fleischman, Paul. 1991. *The Borning Room.* New York: HarperCollins.

Fletcher, Ralph. 1996. *Breathing In, Breathing Out: Keeping a Writer's Notebook.* Portsmouth, NH: Heinemann.

Fountas, Irene C., and Gay Su Pinnell. 1996. *Guided Reading: Good First Teaching for All Children.* Portsmouth, NH: Heinemann.

Fox, Mem. 1988. *Koala Lou.* San Diego: Harcourt Brace Jovanovich.

————. 1990. *Guess What?* San Diego: Harcourt Brace Jovanovich.

————. 1993. *Radical Reflections: Passionate Opinions on Teaching, Learning and Living.* New York: Harcourt.

————. 1994. *Tough Boris.* San Diego: Harcourt Brace Jovanovich.

————. 1998. *Boo to a Goose.* New York: Dial Books for Young Readers.

————. 2002. *Magic Hat.* San Diego: Harcourt.

————. 2004. *Where Is the Green Sheep?* Orlando, FL: Harcourt.

Frasier, Dianne, and Constance Compton. 1994. *Where Is the Cat?* Carlsbad, CA: Dominie Press.

Galdone, Paul. 1973. *The Three Billy Goats Gruff.* New York: Seabury Press.

Greenberg, David T. 1997. *Bugs!* Boston: Little, Brown.

Greenburg, Dan. 1996. *Great-Grandpa's in the Litter Box.* New York: Grosset & Dunlap.

Grossman, Bill. 1996. *My Little Sister Ate One Hare.* New York: Crown Publishers.

Harvey, Stephanie, and Anne Goudvis. 2000. *Strategies That Work: Teaching Comprehension to Enhance Understanding.* Portland, ME: Stenhouse Publishers.

Harwayne, Shelley. 2001. *Writing Through Childhood: Rethinking Process and Product.* Portsmouth, NH: Heinemann.

Henkes, Kevin. 1996. *Lilly's Purple Plastic Purse.* New York: Greenwillow Books.

————. 2000. *Wemberly Worried.* New York: Greenwillow Books.

Hesse, Karen. 1999. *Come On, Rain!* New York: Scholastic Press.

Hill, Eric. 1980. *Where's Spot?* New York: Puffin Books.

Hillenbrand, Laura. 2002. *Seabiscuit: An American Legend.* New York: Ballantine Books.

Holdaway, Don. 1979. *The Foundations of Literacy.* New York: Scholastic.

Johnson, Angela. 1992. *The Leaving Morning.* New York: Orchard Books.

Joosse, Barbara M. 1996. *I Love You the Purplest.* San Francisco: Chronicle Books.

Kidd, Sue Monk. 2002. *The Secret Life of Bees.* New York: Viking.

Kline, Suzy. 1989. *Horrible Harry and the Ant Invasion.* New York: Scholastic.

Krashen, Stephen. 2003. *Explorations in Language Acquisition and Use.* Portsmouth, NH: Heinemann.

Laminack, Lester. 2004. *Saturday and Teacakes.* Atlanta, GA: Peachtree.

Lester, Helen. 1988. *Tacky the Penguin.* Boston: Houghton Mifflin.

London, Jonathan. 1996. *Froggy Goes to School.* New York: Viking.

———. 2001. *Crocodile, Disappearing Dragon.* Cambridge, MA: Candlewick Press.

Loredo, Elizabeth. 2004. *Giant Steps.* New York: G. P. Putnam's Sons.

Lovell, Patty. 2001. *Stand Tall Molly Lou Melon.* New York: Putnam.

Martin, Bill Jr. 1999. *A Beasty Story.* San Diego: Silver Whistle/Harcourt Brace.

Mazer, Anne. 2000. *The Declaration of Independence.* New York: Scholastic.

McDonald, Megan. 2000. *Judy Moody.* New York: Scholastic.

Meckler, Michael. August 7, 2004. "Comics Are Flawed Format to Teach Reading." *The Columbus Dispatch.*

Miller, Debbie. 2002. *Reading with Meaning: Teaching Comprehension in the Primary Grades.* Portland, ME: Stenhouse Publishers.

Mochizuki, Ken. 1995. *Heroes.* New York: Lee & Low Books.

Munsch, Robert. 1985. *Thomas' Snowsuit.* Toronto, Canada: Annick Press.

———. 2001. *Up, Up, Down.* New York: Scholastic.

Nelley, Elsie, and Annette Smith. 2000. *Rigby PM Benchmark Kit.* Crystal Lake, IL: Rigby.

Nikola-Lisa, W. 1997. *Shake Dem Halloween Bones.* Boston: Houghton Mifflin.

O'Neill, Alexis. 2002. *The Recess Queen.* New York: Scholastic.

Oram, Hiawyn. 1998. *Just Dog.* San Francisco: Chronicle Books.

Osborne, Mary Pope. 1992. *Dinosaurs Before Dark.* New York: Random House.

Randell, Beverley. 1994. *Baby Bear Goes Fishing.* Crystal Lake, IL: Rigby.

———. 1994. *The Big Kick.* Crystal Lake, IL: Rigby.

————. 1996. *The Way I Go to School.* Crystal Lake, IL: Rigby.

Raschka, Chris. 1993. *Yo! Yes?* New York: Orchard Books.

Ray, Katie Wood. 2001. *The Writing Workshop: Working Through the Hard Parts (And They're All Hard Parts).* Urbana, IL: National Council of Teachers of English.

Recorvits, Helen. 2003. *My Name Is Yoon.* New York: Frances Foster Books.

Routman, Regie. 2003. *Reading Essentials: The Specifics You Need to Teach Reading Well.* Portsmouth, NH: Heinemann.

Roy, Ron. 1997. *The Absent Author.* New York: Random House.

Russell, Barbara Timberlake. 2004. *The Remembering Stone.* New York: Farrar, Straus and Giroux.

Rylant, Cynthia. 1998. *Scarecrow.* San Diego: Harcourt Brace.

————. 2001. *The Great Gracie Chase.* New York: Blue Sky Press.

Sachar, Louis. 1989. *Wayside School Is Falling Down.* New York: Lothrop, Lee & Shepard Books.

————. 1993. *Marvin K. Redpost: Why Pick on Me?* New York: Random House.

Salem, Lynn, and Josie Stewart. 1992. *Taking Care of Rosie.* Columbus, OH: Seedling Publications.

Shannon, David. 1998. *No, David.* New York: Scholastic.

Sharmat, Marjorie Weinman. 1972. *Nate the Great.* New York: Dell Publishing Company.

Sibberson, Franki, and Karen Szymusiak. 2001. *Beyond Leveled Books.* Portland, ME: Stenhouse Publishers.

Simont, Marc. 2001. *The Stray Dog.* New York: HarperCollins.

Smith, Frank. 1979. *Reading Without Nonsense.* New York: Teachers College Press.

————. 1988. *Understanding Reading.* 4th ed. Hillsdale, NJ: Erlbaum.

Spanyol, Jessica. 2001. *Carlo Likes Reading.* Cambridge, MA : Candlewick Press.

Urmston, Kathleen, and Karen Evans. 1991. *Dressed Up Sammy*. Rocky River, OH: Kaeden Books.

———. 1992. *Sammy at the Farm*. Rocky River, OH: Kaeden Books.

Van Allsburg, Chris. 1986. *The Stranger*. Boston: Houghton Mifflin.

Wiles, Deborah. 2001. *Freedom Summer*. New York: Atheneum Books for Young Readers.

Windsor, Marina. 2003. *Bad Dog Max!* San Francisco: Chronicle Books.

Wolfe, Frances. 2001. *Where I Live*. Plattsburgh, NY: Tundra Books.

Woodson, Jacqueline. 2001. *The Other Side*. New York: Putnam.

Yolen, Jane. 2003. *How Do Dinosaurs Get Well Soon?* New York: Blue Sky Press.

Zolotow, Charlotte. 1995. *The Old Dog*. New York: HarperCollins.